What others are saying about this book

"Over a year ago, Stephan Taeger sent me some of these sermons to read. I am still thinking about some of them today. I can think of no better endorsement than that."

—Anthony Sweat, associate teaching professor
Brigham Young University Church History and Doctrine

"Stephan Taeger has a gift. He has devoted great effort to understanding the art of preaching—without sounding preachy. *Ears to Hear* will immerse you in the scriptures and gospel concepts in a refreshing way that is sure to not only enlighten your mind but also soften your heart. The measure of a truly good book for me is the degree to which I feel inspired and motivated to be a better person. This book not only passes that test but also exceeds it."

—Tyler J. Griffin, BYU Department of Ancient Scripture
Author of *When Heaven Feels Distant*; coauthor of *Come Unto Me: Illuminating the Savior's Life, Mission, Parables, and Miracles*; and cohost of Book of Mormon Central's
Come Follow Me Insights series on YouTube.

"If you want a book where the author tells you exactly what to think, then this book is not for you. But if you want a book full of profundity that engages both heart and mind and leaves you pondering its messages for days, look no further. In this book, Taeger delightfully provokes his readers—almost tauntingly—to engage with his sermons and 'catch' for themselves their transformative meanings. When listening to and reading his sermons, I am almost inexplicably drawn in to a journey of discovery by his concrete images of real life, abrupt scene changes along the way, and unexplained parables. And even though I can't always tell where he's leading me at first, I'm never disappointed with the outcome. I feel nourished by a master teacher who has thrilled me with insight and inspired in me deeper discipleship—all without directly telling me what to think or how to live."

—Scott Woodward, Religious Education, BYU–Idaho

"Stephan has a unique way of capturing and holding the reader's attention as he takes familiar topics and helps us see them in a different light. Full of new parables, insightful questions, and powerful messages, *Ears to Hear* is sure to touch your heart."

—John Hilton III, associate professor, BYU Religious Education

"Elder David A. Bednar once succinctly explained that teaching is not just talking and telling. At the heart of gospel, teaching is the ability to listen to students, discern their needs, and help them engage with the word of God in a way that provides both a meaningful and a revelatory experience. Stephan Taeger has devoted over a decade to researching, practicing, and refining this ability to teach in a way that draws learners into this type of experience. This masterful book contains some of the fruits of his efforts with each chapter beckoning the reader to engage the text of the Book of Mormon in new and profound ways."

—Ryan H. Sharp, assistant professor, BYU Religious Education
Author of *Meeting Christ in the Book of Mormon*

EARS

to

Hear

EARS *to* Hear

STEPHAN TAEGER

CFI

AN IMPRINT OF CEDAR FORT, INC.
SPRINGVILLE, UTAH

ISBN 13: 978-1-4621-3782-4

Published by CFI, an imprint of Cedar Fort, Inc.
2373 W. 700 S., Springville, UT 84663
Distributed by Cedar Fort, Inc., www.cedarfort.com

Library of Congress Control Number: 2020933659

Cover design by Wes Wheeler
Cover design © 2020 Cedar Fort, Inc.

Printed in the United States of America

10 9 8 7 6 5 4 3 2 1

Printed on acid-free paper

For Kirsten

Contents

— ⚬⚭⚬ —

CONTENTS

Acknowledgments

I would like to thank Kirsten for her constant support, love, and encouragement. I am grateful for Jared Roberts, Karina Carson, Heidi Applegarth, Katelynd Blake, Anthony Sweat, Emily Belle Freeman, David Butler, Ralph and Diana Taeger, Mark Applegarth, and my Brambling Brothers for reviewing portions (or all) of my manuscript. I am extremely grateful for everyone at Cedar Fort for their help with every aspect of this project.

Finally, a special thanks to Fred Craddock for teaching me how to hear and be heard.

What Makes This Book Different

―――――――――――――― ∽⊙〜 ――――――――――――――

In 1972, President Howard W. Hunter did something unusual in general conference. He approached the pulpit and said, "Observing the clock, I fold the notes that I have prepared and place them in my inside pocket. But let me take just a moment to mention a little incident that made an impression upon me when I was a boy." President Hunter then told a story of watching a large bird find and eat a worm in front of a baby bird that was "obviously just out of the nest" and "squawking in protest." After the large bird flew away, however, the baby bird found and ate a worm in the same way he had witnessed the large bird find and eat a worm. Without any further explanation, President Hunter concluded by saying, "God bless the good people who teach our children and our youth, I humbly pray, in Jesus' name. Amen."[1]

That was it.

I wasn't alive in 1972, but I have wondered about the conversations on the way home from that general conference. Did everyone understand President Hunter's message? Did parents explain it to their children? What inspired insights did people receive as they pondered his story? Rather than directly stating his message, President Hunter gave his listeners a chance to discover the meaning of the story for themselves. This is often how the Savior taught. He used parables and imagery

―――――――――――

1. President Howard W. Hunter, "A Teacher," *Ensign*, July 1972.

with remarkable economy and depth. As one New Testament scholar explained, a parable works by "leaving the mind in sufficient doubt about its precise application to tease it into active thought."[2]

The mini-sermons I have written in this book try to imitate this same experience. Much of my academic work has focused on homiletics (the art of writing sermons). The specific school of preaching I have studied is often called "narrative preaching." In this style of preaching, messages are stated indirectly in a way that helps learners apply the message to their own lives. In addition, the end of each sermon is left open to encourage the listener to ponder upon the meaning of the sermon.

I recognize that Latter-day Saints don't normally use words like *sermon* or *preaching*. As Elder David A. Bednar explained, the word *preach* can have "some negative baggage associated with it. We think of people ranting and raving and pounding the pulpit; that is not it at all."[3] However, Elder Bednar clarified that "Preaching is explaining and articulating the doctrine of Christ by the power of the Spirit."[4]

It may be helpful to understand that as a sermon develops in this book, ideas are often considered, rejected, or refined in order to move you along to a new insight. Some of these sermons state the message more directly, while others only hint at it. Regardless, these sermons are not written as a smorgasbord of ideas with the hope that you will make some random connection. Instead, each sermon has a specific message that is unfolded in a way to help you make your own discoveries and think differently about a gospel topic.

Of course, the gospel often needs to be stated directly. We should be as clear as possible about what we believe, what we know about our Father in Heaven, His Son Jesus Christ, and the restored gospel. But there are times when it is best to let people discover certain messages for themselves. In the words of Elder Bednar, "The most important learnings of life are caught—not taught."[5]

---

2. C. H. Dodd, *The Parables of the Kingdom*, 3rd ed. (New York: Charles Scribner's Sons, 1958), 16.

3. Elder David A. Bednar, "Teach Them to Understand," Ricks College Campus Education Week devotional, June 1998.

4. Bednar, "Teach Them to Understand."

5. Elder David A. Bednar, "Seek Learning by Faith," *Ensign*, Sept. 2007.

Finding What We Are Seeking

1 Nephi 1:11–15

"I Nephi, having been born of goodly parents, therefore I was taught somewhat in all the learning of my father" (1 Nephi 1:1). How many times have you read that sentence? Those who grow up in the Church start learning the Book of Mormon on the way home from the hospital. In Primary we sing, "I will go, I will do the things the Lord commands!"[6] On Sunday afternoons, Latter-day Saint children watch Nephi cartoons while holding their action figures. Missionaries have Stripling Warrior T-shirts and play "Book of Mormon golf." As adults, we are challenged to read the entire Book of Mormon by different Church leaders throughout our lives. Those who are raised in the Church know Mormon's record from title page to pronunciation guide.

Of course, familiarity with the Book of Mormon is a blessing. We can constantly draw upon its narratives and principles to guide our lives. However, it can also be challenging to connect to a story we've been reading our whole lives. There's only so many times we can act surprised when Nephi shocks his brothers.

How should we read a book that we know so well?

Some take an "apologetic" approach. That doesn't mean we "apologize" for what we believe; it means we defend the faith. Dr. Hugh Nibley

---

6. "Nephi's Courage," *Children's Songbook* (Salt Lake City: The Church of Jesus Christ of Latter-day Saints, 1989), 120.

spent a lot of his academic career looking for evidence that confirms the historicity of the Book of Mormon. His work has blessed the kingdom and even helped some members of the Church strengthen their faith in the restored gospel. Another scholar named Jack Welch found chiasmus in the Book of Mormon as a missionary in Germany in the 1960s. That discovery completely changed the way scholars studied the Book of Mormon. When I was a missionary, I remember watching Daniel Peterson on the documentary *Evidences of the Book of Mormon*. Dr. Peterson lays out several convincing arguments that the Book of Mormon is an ancient American record. Perhaps we could mix up our scripture study by learning these apologetic arguments and making note of them in our Gospel Library app.

In all honesty, I don't think some members of the Church are aware of the richness that comes from occasionally studying the Book of Mormon academically and even apologetically. That kind of precision shows a deep love for the book and provides further context for its life-changing principles. That said, I don't think it's enough. Our spirits long for more than just profundity, nuance, and richness.

We need something more.

In order to have a *spiritual* experience with the Book of Mormon, perhaps we could seek advice on how to improve our scripture-reading skills. Many sources give you suggestions on specific techniques that are intended to enhance scripture study. They emphasize the importance of searching for cross-references, analyzing maps, praying before you read, asking questions of the text, looking for keywords, taking notes, and visualizing the narratives. I think these skills would really help someone get more out of the scriptures. However, there have been times when I feel frustrated because I'm using all the "correct" scripture study skills and I'm still not having the right kind of experience. I know that not every encounter with the Book of Mormon will be life-changing, but focusing on skills sometimes makes my scripture study feel a little mechanical.

I know this much: it is essential that we figure out how to read scripture, because we need to be fed. 1 Nephi 1 records Lehi's vision of God sitting on a throne. In the same vision, Lehi witnessed One descend out of heaven whose "luster was above that of the sun at noon-day" (1 Nephi 1:9). Lehi was then given a book and told to read. As he read, Lehi was "filled with the Spirit of the Lord" (1 Nephi 1:12) and saw "great and marvelous things" (1 Nephi 1:14). In fact, his "soul did rejoice, and his whole heart was filled" (1 Nephi 1:15). That's what people need when they read scripture. But how?

I was once talking to a teacher at EFY, and he told me of a student who had approached him and said, "EFY is my spiritual experience for the whole year." That is a nice compliment regarding EFY, but what does that mean for the young man the rest of the year? I think it means the boy is starving. He needs to eat! Give him some ribs, barbecue sauce, sweet potatoes with marshmallows, green beans with almonds, rolls, and ice-cold lemonade. Speaking of scripture study, President Eyring said, "It's like food—you have to have it. I know that I need the scriptures like I need food."[7]

Unfortunately, when someone is not fed through the word of God, it affects other aspects of their spiritual life. People start wondering why they spend two hours at church every week. They start thinking that watching a good movie is more powerful than the Sermon on the Mount. Spirituality becomes as mindlessly routine as doing the dishes. It's not an accident that those who hold on to the iron rod make it to the tree of life and those who don't wander off into "strange roads" (1 Nephi 8:32). Meaningful scripture study is one of the most fundamental ways to keep our spiritual lives vibrant.

Many would say that the primary way to get something out of scripture study is to apply the word to your own life. They suggest that when you pick up the scriptures, you should also pick up a mirror. One should ask themselves: how does this relate to my future? Can I use this verse at work? Who in my family can I share this scripture with? How would this story help me in my calling? Can this principle help me in my trials?

In other words, when we read about Enos praying in the woods, we are actually learning how to repent. When we read about Ammon preaching to the Lamanites, we are learning how to be a missionary to a group of people who don't want anything to do with the gospel. When we read about Samuel the Lamanite on Zarahemla's wall, we are learning how to stand up for the truth. When we read scripture, we have to ask ourselves, "What is this saying about me?" The scriptures are primarily about us.

---

7. President Henry B. Eyring, "A Discussion on Scripture Study," *Ensign*, July 2005.

Well, I'm not sure about that.

When Lehi was given the book mentioned above, he didn't look for Lehi. After he finished reading, he said, "Thy throne is in the heavens, and thy power, and goodness, and mercy are over all the inhabitants of the earth . . . thou wilt not suffer those who come unto thee that they shall perish!" (1 Nephi 1:14). Later in the chapter, Lehi testified that the things he "read in the book, manifested plainly of the coming of a Messiah, and also the redemption of the world" (1 Nephi 1:19).

Perhaps the story of Enos is actually about the One who can forgive sin. Ammon teaching the Lamanites is about the One who can change hearts. The story of Samuel the Lamanite is about the One who can protect us from evil.

Ultimately, the scriptures are not about us.[8]

A number of years ago, my wife and I attended the play *Savior of the World* in Salt Lake City. The play covers two major events in the life of Jesus Christ: His birth and His resurrection. The final scene of the first half depicts the shepherds coming to see the baby Jesus. In an extremely cautious, humble, and reverent manner, the shepherds slowly approach the infant. This is their chance to be in the presence of the Messiah.

For me, that is scripture study.

8. "Literalism: Isn't the Bible historically unreliable and regressive?" Timothy Keller [Sermon], youtube.com/watch?v=lJ03Qu0YL7g; accessed Feb. 22, 2020.

One True God

1 Nephi 11:16–33

Some commandments are easy to measure: don't steal, pay tithing, don't murder, and marry in the temple. These commandments are simple to determine whether you've been obedient or not. Other commandments are harder to gauge. For example, "Thou shalt have no other gods before me" (Exodus 20:3). It seems like you would know if you worship Thor, Zeus, Baal, Dagon, or God the Eternal Father. But worship is tricky. Sometimes it is unintentional. Jacob said, "Their hearts are upon their treasures; wherefore, their treasure is their god (2 Nephi 9:30). In other words, our gods are the things we set our hearts upon. Of course, there is nothing inherently wrong with having strong emotions for any one thing or person. The problem arises when we seek our *ultimate* sense of worth, identity, security, and purpose from anything but God.

What makes idolatry particularly challenging is that there are many things that are jumping up and down to be worshiped. President Spencer W. Kimball said, "Modern idols or false gods can take such forms as clothes, homes, businesses, machines, automobiles, pleasure boats, and numerous other material deflectors from the path to godhood."[9] Of all the things that President Kimball mentioned, it's particularly strange to picture someone worshipping clothes, but many people draw their worth from their appearance or clothing. In this quote, President Kimball also mentioned homes as a potential idol. In our culture, there is a subtle

---

9. President Spencer W. Kimball, *The Miracle of Forgiveness* (Salt Lake City: Bookcraft, 1969), 40.

feeling that life "will finally be right" when we have a half acre, a three-car garage, and seven bedrooms. In addition, President Kimball added, "Intangible things make just as ready gods. Degrees and letters and titles can become idols."[10] Some worship the identities they give themselves: musician, intellectual, artist, or athlete. None of these are inherently evil, but they are unstable gods. What happens to the young man who plays high school football, gets recruited by a division one university, is drafted by the NFL, and then is injured his second year? If he gets his worth and identity from the title "football player," he will be crushed.

Some gods are more subtle. Rather than worshipping God himself, many find themselves worshipping His commandments. These people often appear to be faithful members of the Church (and actually are in many ways), but their hearts are set upon a list of "dos" and "do nots." Of course, we should strive to keep the commandments, but this is different than getting our worth and identity from our ability to be obedient. Those who worship a list of rules often feel that God is harsh and distant. In addition, since they get their worth from "rule keeping," they become like inspector Javert looking for evidence of other's faults so they feel better about themselves. When they break the commandments, they have a difficult time feeling godly sorrow. Instead, they feel worthless.

Rules are an awful god.

Laman and Lemuel worshipped what is becoming an increasingly popular idol in our day: a god that isn't powerful. After an angel appeared to Lehi's sons and commanded them to try again to obtain the brass plates, Laman and Lemuel asked, "How is it possible that the Lord will deliver Laban into our hands? Behold, he is a mighty man, and he can command fifty, yea, even he can slay fifty; then why not us?" (1 Nephi 3:31). In one sense, it's convenient to worship a god that is not powerful. A weak god can't ask you to do hard things, because he won't be able to help you. But, if God is all powerful, He can ask us to do hard stuff, and He can accomplish His purposes through the small and simple.

---

10. Kimball, *Miracle of Forgiveness*, 41.

And it came to pass that a young woman talked to her bishop about a very complicated problem. After listening to her for a long time, the bishop said, "I think you should attend the temple more."

The young woman left the office thinking, "I feel misunderstood. I think my problem is much more complicated than that."

However, if God is all powerful, what miracles can He perform with something like temple attendance?

Rather than worshipping a weak god, some people worship themselves worshiping God. Jesus told His disciples, "When thou doest thine alms, do not sound a trumpet before thee, as the hypocrites do in the synagogues and in the streets, that they may have glory of men" (Matthew 6:2). Sometimes I finish my personal morning devotional and I feel good because I like *the idea* that I've read my scriptures and prayed. I can check it off. Rather than connecting with God through the Spirit, I feel better about myself.

In a similar way, many people are now beginning to worship the god of "good feelings." They avoid anything that is difficult or boring and instead chase the comfortable. They want a movie, blanket, and carbonation. Ironically, to avoid pain is to suffer. If we avoid the pain of working out, we suffer with an unhealthy body. If we avoid the pain of having difficult conversations, we suffer with superficial relationships. If we avoid the pain of owning up to our mistakes, we suffer for the consequences of our bad choices. Even love requires one to feel pain. When we care about others, we make ourselves vulnerable to the possibility that they might not love us back. Worshipping the god of comfort will prevent us from experiencing authentic joy.

A few years ago, Kenda Creasy Dean performed a study to better understand how teenagers in the United States view God. She said that many teenagers see "God as a 'divine therapist' whose chief goal is to boost people's self-esteem."[11] Of course, there is nothing wrong with therapy. Many people find healing by working through complicated problems with a professional. However, God does not want a segmented, professional, or occasional relationship with His children.

---

11. John Blake, "Author: More teens becoming 'fake' Christians," cnn.com/2010/LIVING/08/27/almost.christian/index.html; accessed February 27, 2020.

Ultimately, idolatry is not a sin because we choose the wrong god in a great eternal guessing game. Idolatry is dangerous. False gods cannot provide a solid foundation during difficult times.

When a woman in her thirties comes home from a date with another guy she is not interested in, sits on the edge of her bed, and listens to the clock tick, where will she turn?

The "nice home" god?

When a family is standing around their fifty-six-year-old father laying on a hospital bed and the doctor enters the room and says, "I'm really sorry, but it's cancer." Where will they go?

A divine therapist?

When the teenaged boy can't overcome his pornography addiction, where will he turn?

A list of rules?

When the couple that has been married for fifteen years begins to feel that the only way they can be happy is to separate, where will they go for help?

The god of fleeting feelings?

Speaking of humankind trying to find joy from something other than God, C. S. Lewis said, "Out of that hopeless attempt has come nearly all that we call human history—money, poverty, ambition, war, prostitution, classes, empires, slavery—the long terrible story of man trying to find something other than God which will make him happy."[12] Humans have always had the tendency to avoid the one true God and have instead worshipped false gods.

---

12. C. S. Lewis, *Mere Christianity* (San Francisco: Harper Collins, 2001), 49.

However, if humankind won't turn to God and learn of Him, that does leave another possibility.

Maybe He would come to us.

After asking to have the same vision his Father Lehi experienced, Nephi was shown "the condescension of God" (1 Nephi 11:25). At the beginning of his vision, Nephi had the sacred privilege of seeing Mary hold the baby Jesus in her arms. "And the angel said unto [Nephi]: Behold the Lamb of God, yea, even the Son of the Eternal Father!" (1 Nephi 11:20–21). God sent us the perfect representation of Himself when He sent His Son. In being born to two relatively unknown parents, surrounded by animals, and placed in a feeding trough, Jesus was beginning to reveal to us the true nature of God. Elder Jeffrey R. Holland said, "It is the grand truth that in all that Jesus came to say and do, including and especially in His atoning suffering and sacrifice, He was showing us who and what God our Eternal Father is like, how completely devoted He is to His children in every age and nation. In word and in deed Jesus was trying to reveal and make personal to us the true nature of His Father, our Father in Heaven."[13]

When we learn about Jesus, our false views of Heavenly Father begin to melt away, and we learn to worship the one true God. The Bible Dictionary defines repentance as "a change of mind, a fresh view about God, about oneself, and about the world."[14] Therefore, when we study the life of Jesus Christ, we are beginning to repent in the deepest way possible. We aren't merely changing behaviors or setting goals, we are *beholding* the nature of God.

Nephi saw that "the Lamb of God went forth and was baptized" (1 Nephi 11:27). Among other things, this experience teaches us that Father in Heaven is a God who keeps His own rules.

---

13. Elder Jeffrey R. Holland, "The Grandeur of God," *Ensign*, Nov. 2003.

14. See "Repentance" in the Bible Dictionary.

Nephi saw "twelve others following" (1 Nephi 11:29) the Savior. When we read about Jesus giving His disciples priesthood authority, we learn about a God who wants to *share* His power.

Nephi saw that Jesus "went forth ministering unto the people" (1 Nephi 11:27). When we read about our Savior taking time for little children, the sick, and the ignored, we learn about a God who is not too busy or important for anyone.

Nephi saw "multiples of people" (1 Nephi 11:31) who "were healed by the power of the Lamb of God" (1 Nephi 11:31). When we witness the Savior stop and minister to the woman with an issue of blood, we see a God who has time for every individual on this planet. When we watch Him raise the daughter of Jairus, we learn about a God who can bring life to anything that is dead.

However, there is one particular moment when the nature of God is most sublimely revealed in Jesus. Nephi saw that Jesus was "taken by the people; yea, the Son of the everlasting God was judged of the world . . . And I, Nephi, saw that he was lifted up upon the cross and slain for the sins of the world" (1 Nephi 11:32–33). Elder Holland said that it is "especially in His atoning suffering and sacrifice"[15] that we learn about the true nature of God our Father. For most of the world's history, people would have been confused about the idea that Jesus suffering, bleeding, and hanging from a cross best represents the most powerful being in the universe.

What does that reveal about God?

On my mission in Las Vegas, I was playing basketball and I accidentally ran directly into a metal volleyball pole that was on the side of the court. I was bleeding seriously enough that the other missionaries believed it would be best for me to go to the doctor. When I arrived, the doctors thought that I should be immediately taken to the hospital. Eventually, an ambulance came, and I was strapped down to a stretcher so my neck wouldn't move. When I was brought to the room where they

---

15. Holland, "The Grandeur of God."

would stitch up my nose, I was surrounded by people who were in much worse shape than I.

At one point, a man who was not moving was wheeled in on a stretcher. He had an oxygen mask on his face, and a crowd of doctors rushed to him. He had been hit by a car. I can still hear in my mind one doctor who kept asking, "Sir, what's your name? What's your name?" He didn't answer.

As I watched the doctors do everything they could to help him, I overheard one doctor say, "When the EMTs put this man into the ambulance, he started punching them." I couldn't believe what I was witnessing. Here was someone who had been fighting against his only source of healing.

The doctors, however, still kept doing everything they could to help.

Throughout time, God has sent prophets to teach us about Him. For the most part, humankind has ignored those messengers. Our Father in Heaven eventually sent His Son to reveal His true nature, but instead of embracing Him, Jesus was put on a cross.

And yet, He still kept loving the very people who rejected Him.

God is like that.

And that is why you and I will have "no other gods."

Entering into the Presence of God

2 NEPHI 16:1–18

Some chapters in the scriptures contain such profound meaning that they are difficult to express in words. For example, how do you really help someone sense the depth of the tree of life? How do you capture the feeling of the First Vision in Sunday School? Which personal experience best illustrates the Savior's visit to the Nephites?

Although not as well known, I think we should add 2 Nephi 16 to the list. It is extremely sacred. This chapter is a story about a prophet who has a direct encounter with the divine. I feel like I need to tiptoe and speak quietly around this chapter.

One reason this story demands reverence is that Isaiah hears the voice of God. In what is often recognized as his prophetic call, Isaiah said, "I heard the voice of the Lord, saying: Whom shall I send, and who will go for us?" (2 Nephi 16:8). Although the calling of a prophet is unique, Latter-day Saints believe that hearing the Lord's voice is something that is available to all. We know that people everywhere can put themselves in a position to hear the Lord speaking in one way or another. President Dieter F. Uchtdorf said,

> He speaks to us everywhere.
> As you read God's word recorded in the scriptures, listen for His voice.
> During this general conference and later as you study the words spoken here, listen for His voice.
> As you visit the temple and attend church meetings, listen for His voice.

Listen for the voice of the Father in the bounties and beauties of nature, in the gentle whisperings of the Spirit.

In your daily interactions with others, in the words of a hymn, in the laughter of a child, listen for His voice.[16]

In this story, however, Isaiah didn't just hear a voice. He saw a seraph with six wings declare, "Holy, holy, holy is the Lord of Hosts; the whole earth is full of his glory" (2 Nephi 16:3). In fact, Isaiah saw "the Lord sitting upon a throne, high and lifted up" (2 Nephi 16:1).

As Latter-day Saints, we believe that mortals can receive visitations from angels and even the Lord Himself. In fact, our history starts with the First Vision—when God the Father and His Son Jesus Christ personally appeared to Joseph Smith. At other times, some of the General Authorities have shared similar experiences with members of the Church. For example, Lorenzo Snow and His granddaughter were once in the Salt Lake Temple when President Snow "held out his left hand and said: 'He stood right here, about three feet above the floor. It looked as though He stood on a plate of solid gold.' Grand-pa told me what a glorious personage the Savior is and described His hands, feet, countenance and beautiful white robes, all of which were of such a glory of whiteness and brightness that he could hardly gaze upon Him."[17]

While visiting the Fort Peck Reservation on Church business, Elder Melvin J. Ballard received a "wonderful manifestation." He said, "I was led into a room where I was informed I was to meet someone. As I entered the room I saw, seated on a raised platform, the most glorious being I have ever conceived of, and was taken forward to be introduced to Him. As I approached He smiled, called my name, and stretched out His hands toward me. If I live to be a million years old I shall never forget that smile . . . I fell at His feet, and there saw the marks of the nails; and as I kissed them, with deep joy swelling through my whole being, I felt that I was in heaven indeed."[18]

---

16. President Dieter F. Uchtdorf, "The Love of God," *Ensign*, Nov. 2009.

17. LeRoi C. Snow, "An Experience of My Father's," *Improvement Era*, Sept. 1933, 677.

18. Elder Melvin Joseph Ballard, *Melvin J. Ballard, Crusader for Righteousness* (Salt Lake City: Bookcraft, 1966), 65–66.

Orson F. Whitney had a vision of the Savior in Gethsemane. He said, "As [Jesus] prayed the tears streamed down his face, which was toward me. I was so moved at the sight that I also wept, out of pure sympathy. My whole heart went out to him; I loved him with my all my soul, and longed to be with him as I longed for nothing else."[19]

In 1989, during general conference, David B. Haight reported what happened to him during a hospital stay. He said, "I was shown a panoramic view of His earthly ministry: His baptism, His teaching, His healing the sick and lame, the mock trial, His Crucifixion, His Resurrection and Ascension."[20]

It's hard to imagine, but Isaiah's encounter went *beyond* receiving a personal visitation from the Lord. In verse 5, Isaiah cried out, "Wo is unto me! for I am undone; because I am a man of unclean lips; and I dwell in the midst of a people of unclean lips; for mine eyes have seen the King, the Lord of Hosts" (2 Nephi 16:5). Following this confession, a seraphim flew toward Isaiah with a live coal in his hand and placed it on Isaiah's mouth! The seraphim then declared, "Lo, this has touched thy lips; and thine iniquity is taken away, and thy sin is purged" (2 Nephi 16:7). More than an experience with his eyes and ears, Isaiah's heart was changed. He received a cleansing of his soul.

After this experience, Isaiah would never be the same.

In the scriptures, when the Savior appears, people's lives start improving. Whether it's the leper, the widow of Nain, or the two blind men, in the words of President Howard W. Hunter, "Whatever Jesus lays His hands upon lives."[21] Something deep inside humans needs direct encounters with God. In a world full of neon signs, high fructose corn syrup, advertisements, digital screens, and twenty-four-hour music, we need to feel the presence of God. Our spirits yearn for concrete spiritual experience. We need more than the excitement of an action movie or sports. We need the divine.

---

19. "The Divinity of Jesus Christ," *Improvement Era,* Jan. 1926.

20. Elder David B. Haight, "The Sacrament—and the Sacrifice," *Ensign,* Nov. 1989.

21. President Howard W. Hunter, "Reading the Scriptures," *Ensign,* Nov. 1979.

And it came to pass that a famous artist lived in a small town. At lunch one day, three teenage boys decided that they wanted to meet the artist. To these young men, it seemed like everyone else had met the artist. First, the boys tried to find him at the art store. When they asked the store owner if the artist had been there, he said, "Yes, he comes here sometimes, but he hasn't been in today." Next, the three young men went to the city park (they thought he might be painting the landscape), but he was not there. After trying the museum, the grocery store, the ballpark, and the city hall, the three boys decided to give up looking for the artist. The next day at the lunch table they were discussing their failure when a fourth friend sat down next to them.

"How's it going? What's wrong?"

"We looked all over town for the famous artist and we couldn't find him."

"I know how to meet the artist."

"How?" the three teenagers asked.

"It's really quite simple, actually. If you want to be with someone, you have to go to their house."

Where does Isaiah's experience take place? It has altars, sacred clothing, angels, the deep cleansing of sin, and the presence of the Lord Himself.

Can you imagine if you lived near a place like that?

One Lesson About Prayer

ENOS 1:12–17

One of the greatest joys of being a parent is listening to your children pray. I once had a friend who told me that his daughter said, "We are grateful for D.I." during a prayer. Based on how much my children say, "Please bless that we will have a great time," my home should feel like the Fourth of July year round.

Once, my wife and I planned to have a family night at the park. We told our children that we could stay until the sun went down. During the opening prayer, one of our sons said, "Please bless that the sun will stay up tonight." Of course, I'm not going to stop my son's prayer and say, "Normally we don't ask for astronomical bodies to stay in their place." It was the simple and sweet prayer of a child.

But at some point, everyone needs to learn certain lessons about prayer.

I was once talking to a young man who had recently returned from his mission. We were discussing his future plans, and he told me that he had made an agreement with God. He was going to do something (I can't remember what his end of the bargain was) and God was going to get him into Harvard Law School. I don't think he had bad intentions, but something seemed off about making a deal with God. The Bible Dictionary says, "Prayer is the act by which the will of the Father and the will of the child are brought into correspondence with each other."[22] When we forget this principle, we end up thinking that prayer is an eternal vending machine.

President Boyd K. Packer's family once had a cow named "Bossy." Unfortunately, the cow swallowed a wire, and the veterinarian said the cow would not live. President Packer said,

> Before I left, we had our family prayer. Our little boy said our prayer. After he had asked Heavenly Father to "bless Daddy in his travels and bless us all," he then started an earnest plea. He said, "Heavenly Father, please bless Bossy cow so that she will get to be all right." In California I told of the incident and said, "He must learn that we do not get everything we pray for just that easily."[23]

Fred Craddock, a preacher from another faith, was once invited to a home with "twelve or thirteen couples" to have prayer and scripture study. Someone at the meeting had been keeping track of answers to prayers members of the group had received. People had received a mink stole, new luggage, a date with somebody named Mike, and a trip to Hawaii. Dr. Craddock said, "I'm a little bothered that these are your prayers in a world anguishing and languishing under oppression and falsehood and poverty and disease . . ."[24]

If someone were to ask me to make a list of words they should remember when praying, I would include the word *caution*. It's too easy to rattle off demands like someone ordering fast food. Today, over eight hundred million people on earth do not have enough food. About ten percent of the world does not have clean drinking water. Should we really pray for new luggage or trips to Hawaii?

But I'm afraid that we might let this truth get in the way of a more beautiful truth about prayer. The story of Enos illustrates that we should be *more* than just careful when we talk to God.

---

22. See "Prayer" in the Bible Dictionary.

23. President Boyd K. Packer, "Prayer and Promptings," *Ensign*, Nov. 2009.

24. Fred Craddock, *Craddock Stories* (St. Louis, MI: Chalice Press, 2001), 32–33.

After praying for himself and his brethren, Enos prayed for his enemies—the Lamanites. In his mind, they were a "wild, and ferocious, and a blood-thirsty people" (Enos 1:20). He said that if the Nephites "Should fall into transgression and . . . be destroyed," he hoped that "the Lamanites should not be destroyed" (Enos 1:13). Enos asked the Lord to "preserve a record of [his] people" by the "power of his holy arm" that would be "brought forth at some future day" so the Lamanites "might be brought unto salvation" (Enos 1:13).

Is Enos allowed to pray like that? Essentially, he is asking God to preserve the Book of Mormon for over a thousand years, orchestrate history so that the record is buried near Joseph Smith's home, provide a way for the record to be translated, inspire missionaries to testify of the Book of Mormon to Lehi's descendants, and help those descendants gain a testimony so they can receive the ordinances of salvation.

Is Enos allowed to be so specific? So bold?

My wife makes the most wonderfully ridiculous birthday cakes. A number of years ago, one of our children asked for a lion cake. So, Kirsten made a lion face cake. Multiple times, she has made football- or princess-related cakes. Once she made a cake in the shape of a number five that was also a racetrack. For one son, she made a train (upright) with cookie wheels, an ice cream cone smoke stack, pretzel sticks as logs, and Kit-Kat bar train tracks. One of our sons once said, "I want a pirate ship *and* a volcano." So, she made a pirate ship (also upright) that had Lego pirates on the deck. Next to the ship was a volcano cake featuring red frosting, candles, and dry ice billowing from the top.

One might ask, "Why on earth would someone make such wonderfully ridiculous birthday cakes?"

I think it has everything to do with who is asking.

Jesus said, "What man is there of you, whom if his son ask bread, will he give him a stone? Or if he ask a fish, will he give him a serpent? If ye then, being evil, know how to give good gifts unto your children, how much more shall your Father which is in heaven give good things to them that ask him?" (Matthew 7:9–11).

It's true that we should be cautious when we pray. But we shouldn't let that get in the way of the fact that God also wants us to be specific and bold in our prayers. When Enos offered a prayer like that, the Lord covenanted with him "that he would bring [the records] unto the Lamanites in his own due time" (Enos 1:16). Enos, in return, said his "soul did rest" (Enos 1:17).

When President Boyd K. Packer told the Bossy cow story (mentioned previously) in general conference, he became full of emotion. He then said, "There was a lesson to be learned, but it was I who learned it, not my son. When I returned Sunday night, Bossy had 'got to be all right.'"[25]

25. Packer, "Prayer and Promptings."

Your Biography

MOSIAH 2:10–15

If you could read a biography about George Washington, Joan of Arc, Mozart, or Emily Dickinson, which one would you choose? All four were remarkable people. Washington led the American Revolution. Joan of Arc received revelations that some believe helped the French win key battles. Mozart was a genius, composing music by the age of five. Emily Dickinson wrote almost eighteen hundred poems and became one of America's most respected poets. If you were to get to know and be influenced by one of these people, which would it be?

I'm not exactly sure why, but there is something about reading the stories of extraordinary people that both inspires and stings. Perhaps when we encounter these kinds of individuals, our own justifications for mediocrity begin to crack. In a similar way, hearing about someone who gets up at 5:45 a.m. to exercise, who always reads their scriptures, and who goes to the temple every week can lead us to think, "Maybe I could do that too."

That is at least one reason to regularly read the scriptures. Not only are we nourished by the teachings of the ancient prophets, but we can also see what humans can become. For example, consider a one-sentence biography of King Benjamin. During his life, King Benjamin eliminated false prophets, fought in battle to defend his people, reigned in righteousness, established peace, and lived in holiness (Words of Mormon 1:13–18). The scriptures are full of people like King Benjamin who are willing to sweat, trek, bleed, speak, and even die for the kingdom of God. As a result, when we read these biographies, our excuses for not doing what we should seem to lose their power. It's hard to complain about cleaning the church after reading about the Anti-Nephi-Lehies. There is less murmuring during Sunday visits when we remember Paul's three missionary journeys.

But I think there is something even more inspiring about biographies. They also demonstrate that each person has the opportunity to make a unique contribution. In the book *The Invention of Hugo Cabret*, two young people are talking, and one says to the other, "I like to imagine that the world is one big machine. You know, machines never have any extra parts. They have the exact number and type of parts they need. So I figure if the entire world is a big machine, I have to be here for some reason. And that means you have to be here for some reason, too."[26] In other words, we probably feel like our life has more meaning and purpose when we begin to discover our unique mission. Otherwise, it's easy to feel like we are just scrap metal.

Few things are more motivating than to read a biography of someone who takes on the mission of becoming an exceptional person. Because these people don't want to live in mediocrity, they use their agency to become extraordinary individuals. Benjamin Franklin was someone who took the project of becoming an exceptional person very seriously. He once made a list of attributes that he wanted to incorporate into his life. He recorded each attribute in a journal and would make a small mark on a page every time he violated that particular attribute. The attributes he chose were

Temperance	Silence
Order	Resolution
Frugality	Industry
Sincerity	Justice
Moderation	Cleanliness
Tranquility	Chastity
Humility[27]	

26. Brian Selznick, *The Invention of Hugo Cabret* (New York: Scholastic Press, 2007), 378.

27. Benjamin Franklin, *The Autobiography & Other Writings by Benjamin Franklin* (New York: Bantam Books, 1982), 76–77.

I would be making progress if I was improving in just one of these areas! Think of what we might become if our efforts to become better were as focused as Benjamin Franklin.

But on the other hand, there might be something that is off in the person who is always trying to become an exceptional person. When one reads King Benjamin's autobiography, it doesn't appear that the purpose of his life was self-improvement. In fact, it seems that self-improvement could just lead to more focus on the self. Consider the parable of Tyler and Ashley who lived in a BYU singles ward:

> Tyler was a returned missionary who woke up every day at 6:00 a.m. to read scripture for thirty minutes. He said meaningful prayers every night. He wrote at least a paragraph in his journal each day and attended the temple once a week. Tyler was a talented basketball player, and he also had developed a unique style of playing the piano. He was well read and fantastic at conversation. Plus, Ashley thought he was exceedingly handsome.
>
> After working up enough courage to finally ask out Ashley, Tyler picked her up from her apartment, and the couple drove to a restaurant to order some food. When the waitress brought their meal, Tyler looked disgustedly at his plate and said, "I told you, I didn't want onions." As the couple was driving home from the restaurant, Tyler recognized someone walking down the road. He said, "I knew that kid in high school. He was such a loser." When Tyler was saying good night to Ashley, the pair noticed an older couple next door struggling to bring in some heavy boxes from their car. Tyler turned to Ashley and said, "See you later!" He then got into his car and drove home.

All of us want to focus on improving, but in one sense, that quest can miss the point. When King Benjamin related his autobiography to his people, he said he had "been kept and preserved by [the Lord's] matchless power, to serve [His people] with all the might, mind and strength which the Lord hath granted unto [him]" (Mosiah 2:11). King Benjamin didn't seek "gold nor silver"(Mosiah 2:12) or put his people in prison. Rather, he taught his people that they "should keep the commandments" (Mosiah 2:13) and he "labored with [his] own hands" (Mosiah 2:14) while he served them.

President Henry B. Eyring said, "Instead of thinking of yourself primarily as someone who is seeking purification, think of yourself as someone who is trying to find out who around you needs your help. Pray that way and then reach out. When you act under such inspiration, it will have a sanctifying effect on you."[28]

Interestingly, one can hear echoes of someone else when they read King Benjamin's biography. He said he was "subject to all manner of infirmities in body and mind . . . consecrated by [his] father . . . King over [the] people . . . suffered to spend [his] days in [their] service" (Mosiah 2:11) . . . "nor [did he suffer] that [the Nephites] should commit any manner of wickedness" (Mosiah 2:13).

> The other day I was walking down a street called "Parable," and I noticed a book on the side of the road. The title read, "A Biography of," but the name was missing. As I flipped through the pages, I discovered a story about a person who had a beautiful home, watched a lot of TV, had his dream job, set a lot of goals, argued with his family, occasionally worked on his calling, and traveled all over the world. I thought, *That's an interesting biography.*
>
> As I walked further down the street, I noticed another book and picked it up. The title read, "A Biography of," but the name was missing. As I began to read, I learned that this person talked with people that others ignored. They didn't worry about money or free time. They prayed often to their Father in Heaven. They were honest. They were kind to rude people. In fact, this person gave their whole life for others. As I closed the book, I thought, *This person reminds me of someone.*

Now, that's a good biography.

28. President Henry B. Eyring, "Surrender to Christ," Ricks College devotional, Sept. 21, 1993. From his book *To Draw Closer to God* (Salt Lake City: Deseret Book, 1997), 110.

Choosing a Story

MOSIAH 10:11–17

There is a lot of debate on how to best understand humans. Some argue that human beings are best comprehended biologically. In other words, if we understand genes, cells, neurons, and the chemical reactions occurring in our bodies, we will know what it means to be a human. Others suggest that human beings are best understood psychologically. Experts in this camp suggest that memory, cognition, beliefs, feelings, and patterns of behavior are the best way to explain why we do what we do. Further still, some people suggest that humans are best explained through their historical or cultural backgrounds.

On some level, all of these explanations help us comprehend the complex beings called humans. However, I personally believe that one particularly powerful way to understand people is through the lens of story. In this view, our lives have a beginning, middle, and end. We have main characters who help shape our personal plot lines. Each of us has moments of dramatic turning points and climactic accomplishments. In other words, you would best understand your grandmother by reading her personal history rather than understanding her culture or knowing her DNA.

Beyond just seeing our lives as one broad story, people also make sense of themselves through the stories they embrace. If a teenaged boy watches a movie about a high school student who eventually makes it to the NBA, he might set his alarm so he can wake up each morning and practice. If a business woman is always reading self-help books that contain anecdotes of people who become wealthy, she may begin to believe that success means making a lot of money. If commercials consistently depict young, beautiful people living in big cities, some people may begin to feel that their personal story is not meaningful because they are middle-aged and live in the suburbs. In other words, we take up our views of the world based on the stories—big or small—we adopt.

In Mosiah 10, perhaps better than anywhere else, we learn the narrative that the Lamanites had adopted. Up to this point in the Book of Mormon, we have mostly heard the Nephite side of history. But this chapter helps us see how the Lamanites saw themselves and their relationship to the Nephites. The Lamanites believed that "they were wronged in the wilderness by their brethren" (Mosiah 10:12), "wronged while crossing the sea" (Mosiah 10:12), "wronged while in the land of their first inheritance" (Mosiah 10:13), and that Nephi "had taken the ruling of the people out of their hands" (Mosiah 10:15).

Suggesting that Nephi had continually "wronged" Laman and Lemuel is a different narrative than what I learned growing up. I used to read Book of Mormon stories for kids with cartoon pictures of Nephi (wearing an orange headband) fearlessly standing up to the never-ending complaining of Laman and Lemuel. But in the Lamanite version of history, the *Nephites* were the wicked ones who usurped the rightful heirs to the throne.

In one sense, this isn't surprising. As Elder L. Lionel Kendrick said, "It has been from the beginning and it will be till the end that the natural man will have a tendency to rationalize and to blame his behaviors on others or on certain circumstances."[29]

For example, a college student who complains to his parents that he could have received better grades last semester if he didn't have roommates who constantly invited people over.

Or the husband who comes home from work, puts down his keys, hangs up his jacket, sinks into the couch, and starts to watch TV. Three minutes later, his wife says, "Don't you think you should spend more time with the kids?" He responds in his mind, *Maybe I would if you didn't bother me so much.*

Or a new family moves into the ward, goes to church for a few weeks, and then stops coming. When the second counselor in the bishopric

---

29. Elder L. Lionel Kendrick, "Christlike Communications," *Ensign*, Nov. 1988.

swings by and asks why they stopped attending, they say, "No one introduced themselves to us."

It is not surprising that the Lamanites had crafted a story that blamed the Nephites—that's the nature of many personal and societal narratives. In fact, the Lamanites had "taught their children that they should hate [the Nephites], and that they should murder them, and that they should rob and plunder them, and do all they could to destroy them . . ." (Mosiah 10:17). The long history of the Book of Mormon consists of two groups of people who are both convinced that they are right and the other is wrong.

Often when we are full of blame, we try to find indirect ways to get others to change. In fact, a few days ago, I was walking down Parable Street again, and I was talking to an ancient Lamanite. He told me about his struggles in dealing with the Nephites. I asked him what he had done to try to make things better.

"Well, we've tried to get justice over and over again."

"Has it worked?" I asked.

"Not really. Sometimes I try to be patient with them, but I just get angrier."

"Perhaps you need to be patient a little longer," I suggested.

"Maybe. I've tried dropping hints about my concerns with different Nephites, but they don't seem to notice. I even bought a book on listening skills, but it doesn't seem to be working."

"What do you think you should do?"

"I'm not sure. I think I will probably just move."

The problem with many endeavors to try to get someone to change is revealed in this quote from David A. Bednar: "It ultimately is impossible for another person to offend you or to offend me. Indeed, believing that another person offended us is fundamentally false. To be offended is a choice we make; it is not a condition inflicted or imposed upon us by someone or something else."[30]

In other words, trying to get someone to change is often flawed, because the problem most usually lies in our offense-taking, not the

---

30. Elder David A. Bednar, "And Nothing Shall Offend Them," *Ensign*, Nov. 2006.

behavior of another. Of course, this doesn't mean we can't be tough with people. In fact, some of the most loving things we can do include telling the truth, correcting someone, defending ourselves and loved ones, and using the legal system to seek fairness and equity. But there is a difference between toughness out of an accusatory spirit and standing up for truth out of a motive of love. It seems backward, but when we are struggling to forgive, we often need to repent.

C. Terry Warner masterfully teaches this concept in the book *Bonds That Make Us Free*. At the end of the book, he tells the story of a woman he counseled who had been abused by her father in the most awful way. In relating the following example, Dr. Warner is not suggesting that we should excuse the misdeeds of others—that would be neither loving nor just. However, real peace cannot come until we learn how to deeply forgive, regardless of what consequences or legal action should be rightfully sought.

> In spite of her efforts, she had gained no fundamental relief, no healing. "I feel as if I am a flute clogged up with sludge. I make all kinds of effort, but no music comes out of me." I asked whether she had forgiven her father. She said she had thought she had but wasn't sure, because she still had no peace.
>
> Then I asked her: "Have you sought His forgiveness for your hard feelings toward him all these years?" She had not. It had never occurred to her to do so. I suggested that forgiveness consists not of forgetting what happened, but of repenting of unforgiving feelings about what happened, and if possible seek forgiveness.
>
> A light went on in her face. She pondered for a few moments and said, "I'm going to do that." The next day she told me she had written a letter to her father the night before, asking his forgiveness. She said, "I saw that by blaming him I was refusing to forgive. I was refusing to admit that he too had suffered in his life and needed my compassion. And now that I have done this, I feel free for the first time in my life. This morning, music is flowing through me and it is sweet." Since that day, this woman has written me letters filled with happiness. In one she said of her father, "Last week I even asked his advice, and he was shocked and pleased."[31]

---

31. C. Terry Warner, *Bonds that Make Us Free* (Salt Lake City: Arbinger Institute/ Shadow Mountain, 2001), 295–96.

There are two stories: one is false and one is true.

One story says, "Your anger, bitterness, and accusations are not your fault." The other story says, "You are free to love all people—even your enemies."

We get to choose.

Proving Your Worth

MOSIAH 17:7–12

One of our sons was once asked to give a talk in Primary, but shortly before standing at the miniature podium, he told my wife that he didn't want to.

"Why not?"

"Because I don't want all the people to look at me."

Maybe I over-analyze things (and when I say maybe, I mean definitely), but incidents like this have helped me see that even at a young age people start worrying about what others think. I don't believe this started unusually early for this child. I think it's just a brute fact that humans seek acceptance.

For example, what happens when there is a knock on the front door and a mother notices toys on the living room carpet, shoes in the hallway, and plates on the end table?

How does the seventeen-year-old boy feel when he is caught singing at a red light?

Or, what is it like for the woman at work who notices her outfit is slightly dated?

Not only are these people embarrassed, but they are also shocked by how difficult it is to stop thinking about their embarrassment!

The need for approval is not just a modern phenomenon. We've seen it affect people in negative ways throughout history. For instance, we see it in the story of King Noah and Abinadi. After King Noah threatened Abinadi with capital punishment, Abinadi replied, "I say unto you, I will not recall the words which I have spoken unto you concerning this people . . . And if ye slay me ye will shed innocent blood, and this shall also stand as a testimony against you at the last day" (Mosiah 17:9–10). Surprisingly, this warning actually shook King Noah. The next verse says, "King Noah was about to release him, for he feared his word; for he feared that the judgments of God would come upon him" (Mosiah 17:11).

When I was speaking at an EFY once, I invited the students to turn to a partner and explain what they would say to King Noah at this moment in the story when his heart was beginning to soften. After letting the students talk to each other, I asked them to share what they discussed. I'll never forget one girl's comment. She said, "I would ask King Noah if he would make this decision if no one was watching." Unfortunately, I think we might know the answer to that question, because "the priests lifted up their voices against [Abinadi], and began to accuse him, saying: He has reviled the king" (Mosiah 17:12). Then "the king was stirred up in anger against him, and he delivered [Abinadi] up that he might be slain" (Mosiah 17:12). King Noah needed the acceptance of those around him so deeply that he killed a prophet.

In a much smaller way, this is like the group of teenagers who decide to watch a movie on a Friday night. About fifteen minutes into the film, some of them begin to notice that the movie is offensive to the Holy Ghost, but nobody says anything, because they don't want to come across as self-righteous.

As we begin to realize all the hurtful, selfish, and shameful things we do (both big and small) simply to feel some form of validation, we can't help but wonder, "How can we overcome this constant need for approval?"

Some people might say we need a better positive self-image. Their argument is deceptively simple: if we thought more highly of ourselves, then we wouldn't worry how others perceive us. We could wake up every morning, look in the mirror, and recite all the reasons why we are amazing. We could put yellow sticky notes around the house that say, "I am awesome" and "I am incredible." Then (the reasoning goes), we would finally have enough self-confidence to do what's right and not worry what others think.

The only problem with this strategy is that it can actually make things worse.

As C. Terry Warner said, "Preoccupation with a positive self-image creates the basis for doubting the validity of that image."[32] In other words, if I try to convince myself of something, I also raise the possibility that it is not true. Elder Neal A. Maxwell put it simply: "Those who are puffed up need constantly to be reinflated."[33]

Well, if inflating ourselves won't help us get over our need for approval, perhaps what we need to do is *deflate* ourselves. We could live a life of service with the hopes that our own problems and self-concern would be minimized. That would definitely help. But how should we make sense of service that's designed to benefit ourselves?

> And it came to pass that a man was feeling bad about himself, so he decided to buy his wife some flowers. After arriving home, the man gave his wife the bouquet.
> She smiled and said, "Thank you, sweetie!"
> The man replied, "*I* was having a bad day so *I* decided to buy you flowers. Now that *I* have bought you flowers, *I* feel much better. *I* have found that when *I* serve *I* am happier."

In moments like this, even service can be soaked in selfishness.

Although simple acts of kindness can probably help shed the constant need for affirmation, I think the problem goes much deeper than finding ways to serve. The need for approval seems to affect our entire lives. No matter how hard we try, we find ourselves wanting to prove our worth to those around us.

---

32. C. Terry Warner, "What We Are," *BYU Studies Quarterly*: Vol. 26: Iss. 1, Article 6 (1986), 51. Available at: https://scholarsarchive.byu.edu/byusq/vol26/iss1/6. Accessed March 9, 2020.

33. Elder Neal A. Maxwell, *Meek and Lowly* (Salt Lake City: Bookcraft, 1987), 85.

In the end, I think we misunderstand the nature of "worth" itself. If we are really going to get over the desire to constantly prove ourselves, we must know what truly reveals the value of a person. Perhaps this parable will help:

> And it came to pass that there was an auction in a small town. The first item for sale was a brown horse.
> "Ten dollars!"
> "Twenty dollars!"
> "Going once. Going twice. Sold!" said the auctioneer. "Wow, that was a low price," whispered the auctioneer to his assistant. The next item for sale was a broom.
> "One hundred dollars!"
> "Two hundred dollars!"
> "Sold to the man in the blue shirt," said the auctioneer. *This town is strange*, he thought. The auction continued in this manner throughout the afternoon. At the end of the day, the last item presented for sale was the Peterson family farm.
> "Fifty dollars!"
> "Sixty dollars!"
> The highest bid was seventy-four dollars and eighty-two cents. "Don't these people know how much this stuff is worth?" said the exasperated auctioneer.
> "The items they bought were exactly the right price," the assistant replied.
> "No they weren't!"
> "They were exactly the right price," repeated the assistant. "Something is worth what someone is willing to pay for it."

The world will put us on trial throughout our entire life. Some way or another, we will constantly feel pressure to prove ourselves. If we are going to erase this need, we can't just be told over and over again that we have worth. We must see and experience this truth deep down in the basement of our souls. We can't just know in the abstract. We need a concrete illustration of our worth. I know it sounds strange, but we need to know what it would look like if someone paid for us.

Fortunately, we can turn to the scriptures and be reminded that:

"They spit in his face, and buffeted him; and others smote him with the palms of their hands, Saying, Prophesy unto us, thou Christ, Who is he that smote thee?" (Matt 26:67–68)

"Pilate saith unto them, What shall I do then with Jesus which is called Christ? They all say unto him, Let him be crucified." (Matt 27:22)

"And when they had plaited a crown of thorns, they put it upon his head, and a reed in his right hand: and they bowed the knee before him, and mocked him, saying, Hail, King of the Jews! And they spit upon him, and took the reed, and smote him on the head." (Matt 27:29–30)

"And they crucified him." (Matt 27:35)

It's not easy to let that kind of love sink in. For some reason, we tend to prevent ourselves from seeing the most important truths. In the last book of the Chronicles of Narnia, Lucy and some of her companions found a group of dwarves who were previously chained up and blindfolded. Strangely, even though they were now free, the dwarves sat in a circle with their eyes closed and their heads to the side trying to listen to what was happening around them. Lucy put some wild violets in front of one dwarf's nose, but he thought it was stable-litter. Suddenly, Aslan appeared, and Lucy said, "Could you—will you—do something for these poor dwarfs?"[34] Aslan replied, "I will show you both what I can and what I cannot do."[35] Aslan growled in their faces and even put a tasty meal in front of them, but the dwarves still refused to open their eyes. "You see . . . they will not let us help them . . . their prison is only in their minds, yet they are in that prison; and so afraid of being taken in that they cannot be taken out."[36]

The chains we feel to constantly try to prove ourselves are an illusion. Our worth is not on trial—it was established two thousand years ago

34. C. S. Lewis, *The Last Battle* (New York: Harper/Collins, 2001), 747.

35. Lewis, *The Last Battle*, 747.

36. Lewis, *The Last Battle*, 748.

when the Son of God "bought [us] with a price" (1 Corinthians 6:20). There is nothing we have done or ever will do that can change the fact that God loves us so much that He sent His Son to redeem us. We don't have to work harder to prove ourselves to any person on this planet. We just need to open our eyes to what the Savior has already done.

This truth can change us deeply.

The person who understands this does not feel the need to drop subtle compliments about themselves.

They don't mind if they get credit when they help out around the house.

They don't have to work themselves up into an emotional frenzy to invite their neighbors to church.

When they are in Walmart, they don't get offended when they over-hear someone say, "Wow, that's a lot of kids."

When their children misbehave in public, they don't feel the need to prove that they are "tough" parents. Instead, they treat their children with kindness and respect, even when they have to be firm.

Unlike King Noah, they are free to stand up for righteousness. In other words, these people rip off the chains and blindfolds. They love God without fear of consequence, persecution, or embarrassment.

Paul said, "Who shall separate us from the love of Christ? Shall tribu-lation, or distress, or persecution, or famine, or nakedness, or peril, or sword . . . For I am persuaded, that neither death, nor life, nor angels, nor principalities, nor powers, nor things present, nor things to come, nor height, nor depth, nor any other creature, shall be able to separate us from the love of God, which is in Christ Jesus our Lord (Romans 8:35, 38–39).

"What shall we then say to these things? If God be for us, who can be against us?" (Romans 8:31).

Raise the Stakes

MOSIAH 28:3–7

I was once talking with someone who suggested that members of the Church should be allowed to sign up for their callings. That seems reasonable, but what if the person who signs up to be ward choir director can't sing or a deacon volunteers to be bishop?

Ironically, to suggest that members of the Church should choose their callings ignores what it means to be "called." Every Kool-Aid-stained face in Primary learns the fifth article of faith: "We believe that a man must be called of God, by prophecy, and by the laying on of hands" (Articles of Faith 1:5). In a world that emphasizes freedom, choice, and personal preference, it can be difficult to remember that we do not pick our callings; the Lord chooses them for us. The night before His crucifixion, Jesus said to His Apostles, "You have not chosen me, but I have chosen you" (John 15:16).

This is extremely comforting. If the Lord selects our callings, we know that he will help us be successful. Lehi needed to know that God was behind packing up the family and walking into the desert. When the new convert is called as Gospel Doctrine teacher, she has to believe that God wants her to teach. The missionary called to a place that he has to look up on a map needs to know that God thinks he can stomach the food, learn the language, and love the culture.

But this raises a question—a question that some may be too afraid to ask: what if you don't like your calling?

And it came to pass that there was a family who moved into a new ward. The father, who loved trees, hiking, fresh air, and fishing, was involved with the Young Men program for most of the twenty-three years they lived in their previous home. Although he was slow to admit it, he had even shed a tear or two each time one of his boys gave a farewell talk to leave on a mission. When the bishopric came over to the house to meet the family, he kept dropping hints about how much he loved the outdoors, leading young people, and the wonderful experiences he had with youth in his last ward. Two weeks later, he was called as ward financial clerk.

One may be tempted to say it doesn't matter how we feel about our callings; what matters is how we serve. On some level, I think that is true, but on another level, how we feel matters—a lot. Even if work in the kingdom is difficult, I think we can still feel meaning and purpose as we fulfill our callings. Of course, there will be moments when we would rather watch Netflix or take a nap, but that doesn't mean we can't have an agency-based desire to bless lives through church service. Work in our callings shouldn't feel like data entry, cleaning the garage, or vacuuming.

Perhaps callings associated with missionary work are the ones that help us the most to get our motives correct.

Once, after having the opportunity to teach some youth, a young man approached me and said, "My friend has a question. He wants to know if he *has* to serve a mission."

That's a tricky question. If I were to say no, the young man might not take seriously the priesthood responsibility (and prophetic injunction) "that every worthy, able young man should prepare to serve a mission."[37] In that sense, the question is like asking, "Do I *have* to obey the commandment to not steal?"

On the other hand, if I answered yes, then the young man *has* to serve a mission. He might look at his mission as some sort of rite of passage that leads to the start of his real life.

To this day, I can't remember how I responded to the question. However, I think the young man's main problem was that he didn't *want* to serve a mission, but he believed that he should. If I were to go back, I

---

37. President Thomas S. Monson, "As We Meet Together Again," *Ensign*, Nov. 2010.

would say, "Yes, it's a commandment, but you might want to work on gaining a desire to serve a mission." Rather than pressure him, I would hope that his heart would somehow change and he would want to teach the restored gospel.

In fact, let's say that I had a chance to talk to this young man for a few minutes again to try to help him gain a desire to go. What could I say? Maybe I should remind him that on a mission, he could learn German, Japanese, or K'ekchi. Maybe I could convince him that missionary work would teach him hard work, how to set goals, and social skills. I might try telling him about the beauty of learning a new culture, tasting foods like Pinakbet, or visiting the Eiffel Tower. Maybe I could guilt-trip him and say, "Don't you love the people of the world?"

It seems like there is something off about trying to convince someone to go preach the gospel in this way. In Mosiah 28, a certain group of young men didn't need to be persuaded to go on a mission. Originally, they were havoc-making teenagers who literally tried to destroy the Church. After an angel appeared and knocked them down, they repented, became Christians, and asked "their father, the king . . . that he would grant unto them that they might . . . impart the word of God to their brethren, the Lamanites" (Mosiah 28:1). They didn't need to be lured into going on a mission, because "They were desirous that salvation should be declared to every creature, for they could not bear that any human soul should perish; yea, even the very thoughts that any soul should endure endless torment did cause them to quake and tremble" (Mosiah 28:3).

In other words, they saw what was at stake.

It's hard to say what I'm about to say. I don't want to pound pulpits and toss brimstone around the room. But some people commit serious sins, and they don't know how to make it right. As a result, they haul around guilty memories that cut into moments intended be filled with peace and joy. Other people fear death. They think the joy they feel when they are with their families will end, the lights will go out, and that will be the end of existence. I know it sounds extreme, but when some people die, instead of ceasing to exist, they will go to spirit prison and experience "weeping, and wailing, and gnashing of teeth." That's actually real; that's what sin does to a soul. In the next life, these people will be resurrected to a lower kingdom of glory. I'm not trying to be negative. They could have been resurrected into the celestial kingdom and enjoyed a fulness of love, freedom, purity, creativity, and union. But God will not force anyone to live a Christian life. He will not eventually compel everyone into His presence. I'm not speaking with hyperbole or using some rhetorical trick. When it comes to missionary work—whether we wear a black name tag or not—the stakes could not be higher.

And it came to pass that there were two missionaries knocking on doors in Louisiana. They walked down a brick pathway toward a house that could appear in a modern-day *Gone with the Wind*.

A man in his thirties answered the door. "Hello Elders!" As the missionaries introduced themselves, two kids ran by with Nerf guns, laughing.

One missionary pointed to a picture on the wall and said, "Is that where you went to college?"

"Yea, I did law school at LSU."

"Where was that picture taken?" the other missionary asked.

"Our family went on a humanitarian trip last year to Africa."

The man's beautiful wife came to the doorway and wrapped her arm around her husband. "How's it going Elders?"

After talking for a few more minutes, the man said, "Elders, we have some friends who are Latter-day Saints. We think what you are doing out here is fantastic, but we are doing just fine. Thanks for coming by."

As the missionaries walked away, a phrase kept circling in their minds: "We are doing just fine."

Is That Enough?

ALMA 15:16, 18

W hen President Brigham Young and some brethren were having a
meeting on the plains during the migration out West, a group of
sisters had an idea. They set up tables and decorated them with "linen
and fine tableware." One account says that "'the fatted calf' was killed;
game and fish were prepared in abundance; fruits, jellies, and relishes
reserved for special occasions were brought out until truly it was a royal
feast." When the more than one hundred brethren finished with their
meeting, they "were led to the surprise gathering, where they enjoyed
a fine meal."[38] After dinner, a violin appeared, and the Saints (which
means "holy ones") began to dance.

This is not how we normally picture the pioneers. We often see them
in blue paintings, dressed in rags, heads down, and covered with snow.
Of course, we need to honor and imitate the endurance of the pioneers,
but if we only focus on stories of sacrifice, I think we unintentionally
communicate that to be spiritual means to be miserable. I remember
seeing people wearing T-shirts around Provo that said, "I can't, I'm Mormon." Some think discipleship means restriction, pain, and boredom.

A number of years ago, President Monson came to the Marriott Cen-
ter and spoke to a few stakes in our area. Although he addressed us for
over an hour, he was funny and edifying. In classic President Monson

---

38. *Teachings of Presidents of the Church: John Taylor*, "Finding Joy in Life" (Salt Lake
City: The Church of Jesus Christ of Latter-day Saints, 2001), 97.

form, he used lots of stories and humor to communicate the gospel. A short time later, I was talking with a member of my stake presidency about President Monson's visit. Without breaking confidences, he told me that someone had approached him because they were a little taken aback by President Monson's talk. This member was troubled that President Monson came across so lighthearted. Why would that person be bothered? I can't be sure, but perhaps they had a certain image of how a prophet should act—one that didn't include a healthy dose of laughter, stories, and fun. Interestingly, Heber C. Kimball described our Father in Heaven in this way: "I am perfectly satisfied that my Father and my God is a cheerful, pleasant, lively, and good-natured Being. Why? Because I am cheerful, pleasant, lively, and good-natured when I have His Spirit."[39] In other words, to try to become like God means to seek after real joy, not spiritual misery.

In fact, there is a certain practicality in how Latter-day Saints view happiness. For us, joy is not a foggy feeling that randomly floats through the window on a Tuesday afternoon. We work for it. Since the beginning of the Restoration, our people have made plans, organized, and built communities where people can experience the peace of the gospel. Zion doesn't appear automatically. We cut down trees and lay brick. In the Church, we have Family Services, Deseret Industries, and the Perpetual Education Fund alongside sacrament meeting, temple worship, and full-time missions. The Lord said in Doctrine and Covenants 29:34, "All things unto me are spiritual, and not any time have I given unto you a law which was temporal, neither any man, nor the children of men; neither Adam your father, whom I created." We want our people to have homes, a job, and food in the cupboard.

Furthermore, while we are taking deliberate steps toward joy, God is raining down blessings and soaking our lives in happiness. We don't need to cover up drudgery with sin. There is plenty that is "lovely, or of good report" (Articles of Faith 1:13) in this world. President David O. McKay said, "Real life is response to the best within us. To be alive only to appetite, pleasure, pride, money-making, and not to goodness and kindness, purity and love, poetry, music, flowers, stars, God, and eternal hopes is

---

39. Elder Heber C. Kimball, *Journal of Discourses*, 26 vols. (London: Latter-day Saints' Book Depot, 1854–86), 4:222.

to deprive one's self of the real joy of living."[40] I know life is full of trials and "growth opportunities," but there really is a lot to be happy about.

For example, I love my community. It's not where I grew up, but Utah Valley has become my home. I love Rock Canyon Park, Provo's Fourth of July parade, BYU Football, and Burger Supreme. I love my neighborhood, lawn, books, grill, guitar, and my easy chair.

But when I remember the deepest kind of joy, I think of people. The group of friends I meet up with once a month or the people in my ward. I think of my family. I love hearing little footsteps in the house (or the silence of sleeping children). I love my wife. She is full of faith and is brilliant and beautiful. There is so much around us to be happy about. Indeed, it's hard for me to see how anyone could have joy *without* their family, home, friends, and community.

That's why I think it's so difficult for many people to identify with Alma 15:16 and 18. They know they are supposed to "liken" scripture to themselves, but they might have a hard time connecting to this story. At this point in the narrative, Amulek had lost everything. He was completely rejected by his community and his family.

How is he supposed to be happy?

When I served on the high council, I heard some missionaries report their missions. I remember hearing one missionary I had known as a teenager. I was impressed with his growth and maturity. After his mission, he seemed happy and whole. As I was listening to him, I began to think about his lifestyle on his mission. For two years, he wore a name tag and a tie every day. He had to be with a companion (someone he had never met before) all of the time. For two years, he had a strict schedule from morning until night. He didn't really have any "me" time. He couldn't watch movies, listen to music, read non-religious books, or hang out with his friends. For two years, he couldn't even spend time with his family. How was this returned missionary so happy?

I think I know why.

---

40. President David O. McKay, October 1963 general conference. See churchofjesus-christ.org/church/news/service-finding-the-real-joy-of-living?lang=eng.

All he had for two years was Jesus of Nazareth.

After Amulek had lost everything, Alma brought him to Zarahemla, "to his own house, and did administer unto him in his tribulations, and strengthened him in the Lord" (Alma 15:18).

You'll have to decide if that's enough.

Mission Statements

ALMA 24

Many organizations align what they do around a mission statement. This allows them to focus all their time, resources, and goals on one unified effort. The thinking goes like this: when the members of an organization know *why* they do what they do, they will be more motivated and make better decisions.

Google's mission is "to organize the world's information and make it universally accessible and useful."[41] McDonald's mission is "to provide a fun and safe environment where our customers can enjoy good food made with quality ingredients at affordable prices."[42] Brigham Young University's mission is "to assist individuals in their quest for perfection and eternal life."[43] *Preach My Gospel* says missionaries should "Invite others to come unto Christ by helping them receive the restored gospel through faith in Jesus Christ and His Atonement, repentance, baptism, receiving the gift of the Holy Ghost, and enduring to the end."[44]

Company mission statements make a lot of sense, but personal mission statements are terrifying. It's hard to define ourselves a certain way.

---

41. See google.com/search/howsearchworks/mission/; accessed March 1, 2020.

42. See mcdonalds.com/gb/en-gb/help/faq/18517-whats-mcdonalds-mission-statement.html; accessed March 1, 2020.

43. See aims.byu.edu/mission-statement; accessed March 1, 2020.

44. *Preach My Gospel* (Salt Lake City: The Church of Jesus Christ of Latter-day Saints, 2004), 1.

By necessity, if we decide what our life is going to be, we also say what we are *not* going to be. Most of us would rather not commit.

However, some people close their eyes, plug their nose, and jump in.

They write down who they are, what they do, and why. President George Albert Smith was one of those people. He wrote a personal creed, a portion of which says, "I would be a friend to the friendless and find joy in ministering to the needs of the poor. I would seek out the erring and try to win him back to a righteous and a happy life. I would not knowingly hurt the feelings of any, not even one who may have wronged me, but would seek to do him good and make him my friend."[45]

John A. Widtsoe was once not very happy with the direction his life was going, so he wrote down seventeen standards he was going to live by. Here are three:

> 8th. That I never do anything that I would not do were it the last hour of my life.
> 9th. That I daily read the word of God, that I may learn his will and that I may be comforted, strengthened and encouraged by so doing.
> 10th. That in any narrations I speak nothing but the pure and simple verity."[46]

As one learns about the mortal life of Jesus Christ, it is easy to tell that He had a profound sense of purpose. His mission seemed to be completely centered around His Father. The first recorded words we have from Him are, "Wist ye not that I must be about my Father's business?" (Luke 2:49). At the beginning of His ministry, the Father declared, "This is my beloved Son, in whom I am well pleased" (Matthew 3:17). When Jesus appeared to the Nephites, He referred to the Father approximately twenty times in 3 Nephi 11 alone! In the premortal life, when the plan of salvation was presented, Jesus said, "Father, thy will be done, and the glory be thine forever"

---

45. *Teachings of Presidents of the Church: George Albert Smith* (Salt Lake City: The Church of Jesus Christ of Latter-day Saints, 2011), 1.

46. As quoted in Elder G. Homer Durham's "Faith, the Greater Knowledge," *New Era*, Aug. 1978, 4–6.

(Moses 4:2). In Gethsemane, when facing the bitter cup of our sins, Jesus said, "Nevertheless not as I will, but as thou wilt" (Matthew 26:39). And, when hanging from the cross, Jesus said, "Father, it is finished, thy will is done" (Joseph Smith Translation, Matthew 27:54).

Ultimately, the Father's will for Jesus was Gethsemane and Golgotha. Every prophet has testified that the Savior was born to give His life. Some personal mission statements include ten-bedroom homes, Caribbean vacations, and "chief executive officer." But not Jesus. His mission was suffering that caused "the greatest of all, to tremble because of pain, and to bleed at every pore, and to suffer both body and spirit" (Doctrine and Covenants 19:18).

If you someday decide to write a personal mission statement that includes something related to Jesus, you might want to keep in mind how He saw *His* mission. If I asked people what it means to be a Christian, they might mention going to the soup kitchen, reading the New Testament, and being chaste.

But following Christ goes much, much deeper than that.

When I think of what it means to be a true follower of Christ, I think of the Anti-Nephi-Lehies. In the same year that King Lamoni's father died, "the Lamanites began to make preparations for war against" the Anti-Nephi-Lehies (Alma 24:4). Rather than fight, the Anti-Nephi-Lehies, who had a history of violence before their conversions to Christianity, held a council and decided to bury their weapons "deep in the earth" (Alma 24:17) as "a testimony to God, and also to men, that they never would use weapons again for the shedding of man's blood" (Alma 24:18).

Many people today would say, "It's not their fault that the Lamanites were acting like that! There is nothing wrong with defending yourself!"

But when the Lamanites prepared to attack, the Anti-Nephi-Lehies went "out to meet" the Lamanites (Alma 24:21), fell upon the ground, and called "on the name of the Lord" (Alma 24:21). In fact, they "praised God even in the very act of perishing under the sword" (Alma 24:23). This proactive decision to embrace sacrificial love rather than force caused the attacking Lamanites to be "stung" with guilt "for the murders which they had committed" (Alma 24:25), leading many to join "the people of God . . . that day" (Alma 24:26).

Is that what it means to be a Christian?

When I consider the story of the Anti-Nephi-Lehies, I'm reminded of what the Savior said to Peter after His resurrection. Jesus told Peter that someday he would be crucified, "signifying by what death he should glorify God" (John 21:19). Then Jesus added, "Follow me" (John 21:19). I also think of Joseph and Hyrum on the way to Carthage, John the Baptist in prison, and Stephen before the Sanhedrin.

Paul said, "Knowing this, that our old man is crucified with him, that the body of sin might be destroyed, that henceforth we should not serve sin" (Romans 6:6).

The world thinks that goes too far.

The elderly couple about to go on a mission for the fourth time might be told by friends, "Hey, don't waste your retirement like that. You should be golfing and visiting grand babies."
Or the Latter-day Saint youth might hear from friends, "You can't give up your high school life! If you keep all those rules, you're throwing away the chance to enjoy life."
Or mothers and fathers subtlety hear from the world, "Having kids takes away your freedom. You shouldn't have to give your life for other people!"

But we hear a different message from the gospel of Jesus Christ.

After being whipped, mocked, spit upon, and given a crown of thorns, Jesus was forced to carry His cross to Golgotha. As Jesus walked, a Roman soldier nearby told a man named Simon of Cyrene to carry Jesus's cross. So Simon picked up the Savior's cross and put it on his own shoulders.

That is every Christian's mission statement.

Past Tense

ALMA 46:38—41

"And it came to pass that there were many who died."

—(Alma 46:39)

I have no idea why Mormon decided to write this verse. There are a lot of "and it came to passes" in the Book of Mormon, but this one seems a little random. It could be that Mormon is simply recording the historical details of that time period. Maybe there is a spiritual lesson here too. He does mention the spiritual state of the people who had passed away. He said, "those who died in the faith of Christ are happy in him, as we must needs suppose" (Alma 46:41).

I guess that's not surprising language for a prophet. They see things from an eternal perspective. But it's also not surprising for anyone who is thinking about death. When we attend funerals, we often find ourselves wondering what has happened to our loved ones. Did they live their lives with sufficient faith? Have they greeted their family members? What are they doing now?

For some, attending a funeral may even raise the question if they themselves are ready to meet God.

On some level, that is a good thing. Many people don't see life from an eternal perspective. They mostly think about the new movie trailer, who the starting pitcher will be tonight, and which clothing stores they should go to this weekend. Of course, these things aren't inherently evil, but they can consume people's lives so that they never really think about eternity, death, or judgment. In that sense, a funeral can wake people up to things that matter most.

On the other hand, death, judgment, and eternity are *always* in the background for religious people. It's not surprising that this was on Mormon's mind. So much of what we talk about as Christians centers on these larger issues. After a Sunday School teacher draws circles on the board to explain the plan of salvation, it seems like most of the questions focus on the spirit world, the kingdoms of glory, or perdition. Even when little kids look at CTR rings, it triggers thoughts about righteousness, blessings, and eternity. Similarly, when Latter-day Saint teenagers walk out the door with a group of friends to get a burger and fries, they hear their mother say, "Remember who you are!" Apparently, mom wants final judgment on her child's mind when they order fry sauce.

Is it healthy to always be thinking about eternity? Of course, we want people to consider the gravity of their decisions. But that doesn't change the fact that for some people it can become extremely taxing. We should try to remember the plan of salvation as much as possible, but what about those who constantly feel guilty when they do?

For example, imagine a young woman who is the Relief Society president in her YSA ward. She writes a thank you card to someone every week, never misses personal scripture study or prayer, and hasn't received lower than an "A" in school since ninth grade math class, but for some reason, she feels sinful and dirty all the time. She carries a microscope around examining every thought, action, and feeling. We certainly want people with unresolved sin to repent, but what about the person who feels guilty almost every time she is reminded of anything related to the gospel?

Maybe we could tell her to read the scriptures, pray, and attend the temple more. Perhaps if she did those things she would feel the Spirit in greater abundance and thus have greater peace in her life. Although I do believe that religious habits are essential to spiritual well-being, I still think it's possible to be participating in these kinds of activities and struggle with unnecessary guilt.

Maybe we could tell her that her sins aren't that serious. We could point to bank robbers, terrorist, and dictators saying, "You aren't nearly as bad as them!" That may be true, but on the other hand, the Savior said in Doctrine and Covenants 1:31: "I the Lord cannot look upon sin with the least degree of allowance." Our sins (even small ones) actually do put us under the influence of evil.

Maybe we could tell her that she needs to forgive herself. I think I understand what people mean by that phrase, but I'm not sure we have authority to forgive our own sins. Dietrich Bonhoeffer said, "Cheap grace is the grace we bestow on ourselves."[47]

Maybe we could tell her that she needs to remember that our role is to do what we can and then let Christ make up the difference. Again, that's true, but who does their best all the time? We understand that the Savior accepts our best efforts when we are moving in the right direction, but why do some fully active, temple recommend carrying, stake conference attending, members of the Church still suffer from feeling unclean?

> And it came to pass that a couple fell in love. After dating for ten months, they took engagement pictures, selected a cake, and chose a reception hall. The couple had a beautiful sealing ceremony, went on a honeymoon, and moved into their new apartment to begin life together. The first week in their new ward, the bishop approached the couple and introduced himself.
>
> The husband responded by saying, "Hi, I'm Sam. This is my wife Brittany . . . well, if we don't do anything to get a divorce." Brittany and the Bishop had confused looks on their face.
>
> A few months later, Sam was walking down the street when he saw an old friend. "Hey Sam! I heard you are married!"
>
> "Well, if I keep trying my hardest," said Sam.
>
> His friend paused and said, "Yea, I guess that's true."
>
> While at Brittany's parents' house for Christmas, the family gathered to take a picture in front of the fireplace.
>
> The father said to Sam, "Come over here. You are part of the family now."
>
> "I better not," said Sam, "You never know what might happen."
>
> "What do you mean?" Said Brittany's father, turning red.
>
> "We are only going to stay together forever if we stay faithful," responded Sam. The family didn't know what to say.

One time when I was attending a religion department faculty meeting at BYU, I heard a closing prayer that I will never forget. The prayer

---

47. Dietrich Bonhoeffer, *The Cost of Discipleship* (London: SCM Classics, 2001), 4.

was surprising in two ways. First, the professor became emotional and usually professors don't have feelings. Second, during the prayer, this man said, "We thank thee that Thou has redeemed us." I was taken aback. Is he allowed to say it like that? Can he say "redeemed" in the past tense?

The prophets in the Book of Mormon think it's okay to talk like that. When Nephi was closing up his portion of the small plates, he spoke of Jesus having "redeemed [his] soul from hell" (2 Nephi 33:6). When Alma woke up after he was struck down for three days, he said, "My soul hath been redeemed" (Mosiah 27:29). When King Lamoni's wife experienced a dramatic conversion, she said, "O Blessed Jesus, who has saved me from an awful hell!" (Alma 19:29). And in the moment when Mormon brought up the fact that many Nephites had passed away, he said they died "firmly believing that their souls were redeemed by the Lord Jesus Christ; thus they went out of the world rejoicing" (Alma 46:39).

Often in the Church, we focus on sanctification, the process of becoming more like God. But we also believe in justification (Doctrine and Covenants 20:30), which Elder D. Todd Christofferson described as being "pardoned."[48] In other words, those who are exercising faith in Jesus Christ, repenting of their sins, striving to keep their covenants, and experiencing the Holy Ghost are redeemed. Past tense.

When we have that kind of confidence in the redemption we have already received, our hearts break with gratitude. We read the scriptures and are reminded of the forgiving love of Christ. Our prayers are filled with praise and worship. We can't wait to share the message of redemption with our friends. We sing hymns at church with our whole souls. We find ourselves having charity for others because, like President Henry B. Eyring said, "Gratitude for the remission of sins is the seed of charity, the pure love of Christ."[49]

On the other hand, it can be difficult to accept the gift of the Atonement. Receiving a gift can be extremely challenging. In fact, I think (and I'm not trying to be extreme) sometimes it is the hardest thing in the world. If we take a free gift from someone, we might have to have kind feelings toward the person who gave us the gift. It may mean we were

---

48. Elder D. Todd Christofferson, "Justification and Sanctification," *Ensign*, June 2001.

49. President Henry B. Eyring, "Remembrance and Gratitude," *Ensign*, Nov. 1989.

wrong about the person who gave us the gift. If we take the gift, we might have to give to others now.

Jean Valjean was brought back by the police to face the bishop he had stolen from. He was completely shocked, however, when the bishop told the police that he had given Jean Valjean the items he took.

Then the Bishop offered Jean Valjean one the hardest gifts to accept:

> The Bishop approached him, and said, in a low voice . . . "Jean Valjean, my brother, you belong no longer to evil, but to good. It is your soul that I am buying for you; I withdraw it from dark thoughts and from the spirit of perdition, and I give it to God!"[50]

Later in Les Miserables, Victor Hugo says Jean Valjean "could not have told whether he were touched or humiliated."[51] In some sense, if Jean Valjean received grace from the bishop, all his excuses for living a bitter, sinful, self-centered life would begin to melt like ice on a July sidewalk.

Sometimes it's the hardest thing in the world to take a free gift.

---

50. Victor Hugo, *Les Miserables* (Hertfordshire, England: Wordsworth Editions Limited, 1994), 73.

51. Hugo, *Les Miserables*, 73.

Practicing in Church

HELAMAN 14:1–13

I believe in the power of words. I know that our world is soaked in pictures, screens, and PowerPoint, but nothing can compare with words. A person at a pulpit with the scriptures in their hands and fire in their hearts still changes lives. I remember once sitting in a priesthood meeting on a Sunday night, listening to my stake president preach on John 8. It was at a time in my life when I felt rather inadequate. After going through the story of the woman taken in adultery, my stake president expressed the idea that God was not "out to get us." Instead, he taught boldly that the Lord was on our side. As I sat among a large crowd of priesthood brethren, I felt like that message was designed for me.

Words are not just sound waves—they change people. Whenever Elder Jeffrey R. Holland approaches the pulpit in general conference, Church members straighten up in their seats and ready themselves for an experience. That kind of preaching can lead us to confess to a family member, set an appointment to visit someone in the hospital, or decide to get up a little earlier to study the scriptures.

In some ways, I think listening to Samuel the Lamanite would be like listening to Elder Holland. In this chapter, we see that Samuel demonstrated very effective communication skills as he described the signs attending the birth of the Savior. Samuel can preach! For example, one of the first things you notice when reading Samuel is that he was specific. He didn't use a lot of bland general words that taste like rice with no butter. Instead, Samuel said, "There shall be great lights in heaven" (Helaman 14:3), "There shall a new star arise, such an one as ye never have beheld" (Helaman 14:5), and "Ye shall be amazed, and wonder" and "fall to the earth" (Helaman 14:7). In addition, Samuel probably offered one of the most specific prophecies in history: "Behold, I give unto you a sign; for five years more cometh, and behold, then cometh the Son of God" (Helaman 14:2). Besides putting a deadline on a prophecy (which would have certainly carried some urgency), this kind of specificity makes Samuel's teaching more vivid. When the Savior described the prodigal returning home, he painted the picture of a boy who was given a robe, shoes, and a ring. With those kinds of specifics, you can smell the fatted calf roasting on the fire. It is often better to create an image rather than to use abstract words. A Sunday School teacher could analyze "faithfulness" for fifteen minutes, or they could describe a mother of four folding the last piece of laundry, helping the kids brush their teeth, finally slipping into bed, and then remembering that she hadn't read her scriptures. We *experience* something as the teacher tells us about this woman getting up, turning on the light, and reaching for the Book of Mormon. A specific image does more to the heart than the word *faithfulness*.

Another aspect of Samuel's preaching that made it so effective was its depth. Samuel said that the Savior would come to the earth and that there would "be one day and a night and a day, as if it were one day and there were no night" (Helaman 14:4). I can't be positive, but I think we can assume that Samuel realized the power of this symbol: Jesus, the light of the world, brings light to the world. Perhaps one reason this symbol is so poignant is that Samuel doesn't explain it. Explaining a symbol takes away the chance for the listener to figure it out for himself. It's like explaining a joke.

The most powerful dimension of Samuel's teaching style was his ability to testify of the Lord Jesus Christ. He said, "If ye believe on his name ye will repent of all your sins, that thereby ye may have a remission of them through his merits" (Helaman 14:12). Our spirits long for the kind of love only the Savior can offer. In a world where we feel shame, guilt, and embarrassment because of our sins and weakness, we need to be reminded that we are loved by One willing to bear our shame, guilt, and embarrassment. When a teacher testifies of the Savior in a way that is insightful and sincere, it's like pouring gasoline on the pulpit.

After analyzing Samuel's preaching methods, it's shocking to realize that some of the Nephites didn't like his message. In fact, they tried to kill him.

Did he prophesy of things that were too incredible for some to believe? Perhaps.

Were the people too hard-hearted? Probably.

Interestingly, Samuel told the Nephites why they had such a hard time listening to him.

He said, "And now, because I am a Lamanite . . ." (Helaman 14:10).

There was once a man named Robert who paid three thousand dollars to attend a business conference. He read the materials beforehand and designed a plan to apply what he learned. When the morning came and Robert attended the first session, he found that he was really bothered by the presenter because he acted like he knew everything. Robert thought, *Doesn't this presenter know that you should be humble when you teach?* During the second session, Robert started looking at his phone and quietly said to himself, "None of this applies to me. The best teachers are relevant! Even I know that!" During the last session, Robert actually had to leave the room because he was annoyed by the presenter's loud voice. He thought, *I don't have time for this.* When he arrived home, his wife asked how the conference went.

"I didn't get much out of it. I was so annoyed by everyone's presentation skills I couldn't concentrate. It seemed like they didn't know even the most basic stuff about teaching."

His wife laughed. Then she jokingly (and a bit sarcastically) said to her husband, "It's really hard to listen to someone teach when you think you're better than they are."

I have studied about how to train and teach people. I'm going to save you the tuition and time. Among the most important aspects of instruction are (1) showing someone how to do something and (2) letting them practice.

"Here's how you throw a football. Now you try."

"Here's how you bake a cake. Now you try."

"Here's how you change a tire. Now you try."

I can think of at least one exception though. When we're in church and someone is teaching about Christianity, we get to practice right then and there.

Life as Christmas

3 Nephi 1:1–13

I'm not sure, but I think I know what makes Christmas so enjoyable.

Anticipation.

When you're a child you can't wait for sledding, hot chocolate, and Santa's arrival. When you're an adult, you look forward to a month of traditions, family time, and an increased measure of the Spirit. In my family, I grew up celebrating Advent every Sunday leading up to Christmas. My father is German, so we put real candles on the Christmas tree. I think my favorite part of December is sitting in the living room with my family, surrounded by Christmas decorations, listening to holiday choral music.

I wait for that every year.

Humans are built to anticipate. Fred Craddock said, "Anticipation enables us to ride out the storm, endure periods of pain and privation, stick with distasteful and boring tasks, maintain sanity in chaos, and survive disappointments and delays in pursuit of our goals. In addition, it is probably the human spirit's greatest source of pleasure, often exceeding that provided by fulfillment of one's anticipation."[52] For some reason, the

52. Fred Craddock, *Preaching* (Nashville: Abingdon Press, 1985), 166.

waiting can be more exciting than the actual event we are waiting for. Which day is more enjoyable: December 23 or December 28?

Christmas-like anticipation shows up in many areas of our lives. College football fans wait all summer, excitedly watching interviews with coaches and players. The sports writers analyze everything from the team's new helmets to the effect the new concession stands might have on the quarterback. On the Tuesday before the first game of the year, people are already deciding what they are going to eat, who they are going to invite, and which T-shirt they will wear. People love to anticipate.

Or, on a summer night, you might find people dressed up as Han Solo, C3PO, or Darth Vader at a movie theater. For ten hours, they switch between standing and sitting in line. Every few minutes you hear the smack of plastic lightsabers or Chewbacca growls. In fact, you might see a line like this not only for the new Star Wars movie, but also for the new Star Wars trailer! People love to anticipate.

Or, on an airplane, a young man sits wearing a suit and a name tag. He has just spent two years in Brazil, and he's about twenty minutes away from landing in Salt Lake City. A certain special girl is waiting with the missionary's family. The girl has a sign that says, "Welcome Home."

Whether it's sports, a new movie, or a special someone—humans love to anticipate.

But not everyone.

It's hard for some of us to comprehend, but rather than anticipating anything, some people's lives are full of dread. They feel like Sisyphus (from the Greek myth) who was punished to continually roll a boulder up a mountain only to watch it roll down again. Sisyphus's life was condemned to be the same thing over and over again, without any meaningful expectation. Interestingly, in Dante's *Inferno*, the sign over the entrance to Hell reads, "Abandon all hope ye who enter here."[53]

A missionary saves up his whole life to go on a mission. He buys suits, gets a missionary plaque, gives his farewell talk, goes to the MTC, but

---

53. From the 1814 translation of Dante Alighieri's *Divine Comedy* by the Reverend H. F. Cary. See also Dante Alighieri's *The Divine Comedy*, translated by C .H. Sisson (New York: Oxford University Press, 1980), 56.

things start to get complicated when he enters the field. Three months into his mission, he begins to think his depression is too much to handle, and after counseling with the mission president, he decides to go home. As he packs his bags, awful and untrue thoughts start to enter his mind: *What do I have to look forward to now?*

The adversary wants us to think that there is no reason to have hope. He wants us to think that something has happened that has permanently changed the future. It's like the newly married couple who get into their first fight. It's not pretty: yelling, tears, and pride. As the wife falls asleep that night, a thought pops into her mind: *How will our marriage ever be the same?* That kind of thinking is not from God. It's like the elder's quorum president who is messing around on the internet one afternoon and comes across a website about the Church. He reads something about Joseph Smith that he has never heard before and thinks, "How can I ever believe in the Church the same way again?"

In 3 Nephi 1, the believing Nephites began to hear challenges to their faith. Some detractors were saying, "Behold the time is past, and the words of Samuel are not fulfilled; therefore, your joy and your faith concerning [the birth of Christ] hath been vain"(3 Nephi 1:6). The text continues: "And it came to pass that they did make a great uproar throughout the land; and the people who believed began to be very sorrowful, lest by any means those things which had been spoken might not come to pass" (3 Nephi 1:7).

What should someone say to another person in that kind of situation? What do the believing Nephites need to hear?

I'm not exactly sure, but I think I would say something like this: I know there doesn't appear to be any possible or reasonable or logical way to believe things will get better. But somehow, someday, the Savior will show up and make things right.

I've seen it with my own eyes.

I once had a student approach me and say, "Brother Taeger, I really struggle with doubt." I told him about a book that addresses that particular trial. He read it and later came to me and said, "I don't struggle with doubt anymore." I've seen people leave the darkest addictions, become active in the Church, and be sealed for time and all eternity. I know people who have struggled with mental illness find real and authentic joy.

We can all be confident that someday we will hear something like Nephi heard: "Lift up your head and be of good cheer; for behold, the time is at hand, and on this night shall the sign be given, and on the morrow come I into the world" (3 Nephi 1:13). If Jesus Christ was willing to come into the world to suffer for your sins, you can be sure that He will come into your life to make things right.

And it came to pass that a woman went to the bishop's office in tears. Her husband just left for another woman, and he's never coming back. The woman doesn't have a job, she never finished school, and she has five kids at home. After listening for fifty minutes, the bishop looked at her and said, "I promise that things will get better. Completely better. Somehow, someday."

Do you think that's true?

Is that just wishful thinking?

Or does she have permission to anticipate?

In Good Company

3 Nephi 12:1–12

The Beatitudes seem backward. How could someone be "blessed" if they are poor in spirit or mourning? The Beatitudes sketch the surprising image of true Christian discipleship. With each verse, another spot on the canvas is painted.

So, what does the picture look like?

A lot of people in Utah want to be Christlike. Maybe if we wanted to show others the image of true discipleship, we could put someone on a plane and fly them to the beehive state. After our guest gets off the plane, looks around at the mountains, and sees the skiing advertisements, we should welcome them with a huge helping of carrot-filled Jell-O. The person will probably still be hungry, so we would need to feed them funeral potatoes covered in fry sauce.

Next, we could drive back to your house and introduce them to your niece who (of course) just got married. Our guest would probably ask her, "How did you meet your husband?"

"Well, I first saw him at BYC, and then we happened to go to EFY together. While at EFY, I was reading the JST, and I decided that I always want to CTR by marrying an RM. So, I sent him off to the MTC, and we met later at BYU, and tonight we are having FHE."

The next day we could bring our guest to church. After going to a Latter-day Saint worship service, he would surely have questions:

"Why are there so many minivans in the parking lot?"

"How come your church is so loud even though you don't have drums or clapping?"

"How do I get *my* church to have a steak conference?"

I think we can do better at showing someone what a true disciple of Jesus Christ looks like—although, that is not an easy task. Sometimes people try to do what's right, but they miss the mark. A family moves into a neighborhood, and seventy-six members of the ward show up to help unpack the moving truck. After kindly rejecting an invitation to church, the family doesn't get any more visits from Latter-day Saints. I don't think that's part of the picture of discipleship.

Fortunately, we have a list. The Savior says it's a list of "blessedness."

A man is reading the Book of Mormon and thinks, *I'm not where I need to be in my life. I need God's help to be better.* "Blessed are the poor in spirit who come unto me, for theirs is the kingdom of heaven" (3 Nephi 12:3).

A woman is looking at the news and feels sick to her stomach as she reads of genocide in a faraway country. "Blessed are all they that mourn, for they shall be comforted" (3 Nephi 12:4).

An elderly man is respectful and gentle to the snappy teenager taking his order. "Blessed are the meek, for they shall inherit the earth" (3 Nephi 12:5).

A woman gives a little extra in fast offerings. "Blessed are all they who do hunger and thirst after righteousness, for they shall be filled with the Holy Ghost" (3 Nephi 12:6).

A girl in college overhears her roommates talking about her. She decides to not take offense. "Blessed are the merciful, for they shall obtain mercy" (3 Nephi 12:7).

A woman sees an older sister from her ward approaching her at the grocery store. She knows if she stops and talks to her it will be at least fifteen minutes. Then she finds herself actually interested in the older woman's life. "Blessed are all the pure in heart, for they shall see God"

(3 Nephi 12:8). Or, like Harold B. Lee said, "In a lesser degree, will you be able to see the 'God' or good in man and love him because of the goodness you see in him?"[54]

Two brothers have not talked in twenty years. At a family reunion, their sister patiently tries to get them to spend time together. "Blessed are all the peacemakers, for they shall be called the children of God."

The Bible Dictionary says something interesting about the Beatitudes: "Rather than being isolated statements, the Beatitudes are interrelated and progressive in their arrangement."[55] If the Beatitudes are a flight of stairs, then the top step is quite surprising: "Blessed are all they who are persecuted for my name's sake" (3 Nephi 12:10).

That's the top of the list?

Joseph Smith walked out of the Sacred Grove and a Methodist minister "treated [Joseph's] communication not only lightly, but with great contempt, saying it was all of the devil" (Joseph Smith—History 1:21). On March 24, 1832, a mob pulled Joseph Smith out of his house and tarred and feathered him. The door was left open, and Joseph's newly adopted son caught a cold, the effects of which later caused the baby to die. In the winter of 1838–39, Joseph Smith was in Liberty Jail while the Saints (including his family) were forced to leave their homes in Missouri. On June 27, 1844, Joseph and Hyrum Smith were murdered in Carthage Jail.

But the scripture says, "Blessed are all they who are persecuted" (3 Nephi 12:10).

A group of men at work show a new hire a YouTube video. He says, "I would prefer not to watch this." His coworkers raise condescending eyebrows and walk out of the room. But the scripture says, "Blessed are all they who are persecuted."

---

54. *Teachings of Presidents of the Church: Harold B. Lee* (Salt Lake City: The Church of Jesus Christ of Latter-day Saints, 2000), 202.

55. See "Beatitudes" in the Bible Dictionary.

An older sister goes to minister to a less-active woman in her twenties. For the seventeenth month in a row, the woman in her twenties stands at the door and gives a ridiculous excuse why the older woman can't come inside. As the older woman walks away, she can hear people inside the house laughing. But the scripture says, "Blessed are all they who are persecuted."

At Thanksgiving dinner, same-sex marriage comes up, and one family member says, "I believe in traditional marriage."

A sister-in-law replies, "I think you are a hateful person."

But the scripture says, "And blessed are ye when men shall revile you and persecute, and shall say all manner of evil against you falsely, for my sake; For ye shall have great joy and be exceedingly glad, for great shall be your reward in heaven; for so persecuted they the prophets who were before you" (3 Nephi 12:12).

And it came to pass that a man died and started walking through the halls of spirits. One hall had pictures of CEO's, oil investors, and stockbrokers. This hall was titled, "The Wealthy." One hall had pictures of paleontologists, physics professors, and neuroscientists. This hall was titled, "The Intelligent." One hall had pictures of skydivers, bike riders, and beach sitters. That hall was titled, "Those Who Had Fun." One hall had impressionist painters, silent film directors, and country singers. That hall was titled, "The Artists." After turning a corner, the man found a hall with some familiar faces labeled, "Christians." It had a picture of Daniel in the lion's den, Paul on his way to Rome to stand trial, and Abinadi in front of King Noah. Then the man found the most curious thing: he found an empty picture frame.

You wouldn't believe who that frame is for.

Do not be afraid.

Family First

3 NEPHI 16:1–3

When I came to Utah my freshman year of college, I had an institute teacher who changed my life. He taught the gospel with such great enthusiasm that I was a GlowStick by the end of class. He was funny, interesting, and powerful, and it was easy to tell that he lived the gospel he preached. I still draw upon his doctrinal insights when I teach my classes. Having the opportunity to be his student was one of the turning points in my life.

After taking this teacher's class a few times, I began noticing some unique things about his family life. I remember hearing that his family was divided up into committees, with each member of the family heading up a committee that consisted of every other member of the family. In fact (if I remember correctly), under that family committee system, one of the children organized a Hawaiian vacation. His family also had a monthly theme that would become the basis for FHE and other gospel study. Every general conference his family had a breakfast of crepes with syrup, strawberries, and whipped cream, because my teacher wanted his family to know that general conference tasted "sweet." Over the years, I've tried to use his family as the model for my own family.

I am always so impressed with people who can organize their life around their family. That's not easy. The minivan needs to be vacuumed, the garage needs to be organized, there's no milk in the fridge, and there is a college football game on TV tonight. I have deep respect for someone who has learned to say "no" to good things in order to say "yes" to their family. For example, I once taught three children of the same family whose father would make them a hot breakfast every morning. I also remember hearing a preacher of another denomination say that his goal was to try to connect with his family every night after dinner. Stephen Covey's family developed a mission statement that was a source of vision and inspiration for many years. That kind of diligence is extremely inspiring to me.

Some people give up their excuses, admit they focus on the wrong things, and start putting their energy into their family. They learn what is at stake and start to believe President Henry B. Eyring when he said, "The greatest joys and the greatest sorrows we experience are in family relationships."[56] They also accept this foundational truth from the family proclamation: "The family is central to the Creator's plan for the eternal destiny of His children."[57] President Boyd K. Packer once said, "The ultimate end of all activity in the Church is that a man and his wife and their children might be happy at home."[58]

> And it came to pass that a family woke up for scripture study. After having breakfast together and quickly planning out their day, the father went to work, the older children went to school, and the mother stayed home with the younger children. During the day, the mother read to the children, brought them to the park, and told them stories about their ancestors. After school, the older children came home and immediately did their chores and finished their homework. At 5:45 p.m., the father arrived home from work to find his family standing in the kitchen laughing and helping to prepare dinner. About seven minutes after sitting down to eat, the family heard a knock on the door. The slightly awkward neighborhood kid asked if one of the children could come outside and play. It was obvious to the dad that this neighborhood friend really wanted to come in and eat.
>
> "Sorry," said the dad. "We are having dinner."
>
> That night, after helping with homework, the mother received a text from her Relief Society president.

---

56. President Henry B. Eyring, "Our Perfect Example," *Ensign*, Nov. 2009.

57. "The Family: A Proclamation to the World" (Salt Lake City: The Church of Jesus Christ of Latter-day Saints, 1995), *Ensign* or *Liahona*, Nov. 2010, 129.

58. President Boyd K. Packer, "The Power of the Priesthood," *Ensign*, May 2010.

"Can you come do a visit with me real quick? Sister Thompson is in the hospital."

"Sorry, I've got to put the kids to bed."

The next day (Saturday) the family woke up and went through their routine. They noticed on the calendar that there was a youth service project at the church. The ward was making humanitarian kits, but the family decided to go boating. They had a great time.[59]

Of course, our primary concern is with our families. But 3 Nephi 16:1–3 expands our view. Jesus had just told the Nephites that they were the "other sheep" spoken of in John 10. Then the Savior said, "I say unto you that I have other sheep, which are not of this land, neither of the land of Jerusalem, neither in any parts of that land round about whither I have been to minister" (3 Nephi 16:1).

Someone may wonder, "Why does this matter? Why do I have to know about 'other sheep'? Isn't that something that strange people spend their time speculating about? I need to focus on my family, my calling, my job, my neighborhood!"

Then the Savior said, "[These lost tribes] shall hear my voice, and shall be numbered among my sheep, that there may be fold and one shepherd" (3 Nephi 16:3). In other words, Jesus of Nazareth wants every person on this planet to become a covenant member of the family of God. Of course, our primary concern is with our own individual families, but Joseph Smith said, "A man filled with the love of God, is not content with blessing his family alone, but ranges through the whole world, anxious to bless the whole human race."[60]

When a young Thomas S. Monson was assigned to minister to the Polynesian islands, he would sometimes stay with a family who lived outside of Hamilton, New Zealand. This family had a son named Mark who collected stamps. When President Monson would come to the family's home, he would bring stamps from the mail "he received at his office

---

59. Based on a parable I published in "The Word Made Flesh: Teaching the Gospel Concretely," *Religious Educator* 18, no. 1 (2017), 48–61.

60. The Prophet Joseph Smith, "Extract from an Epistle to the Elders in England," *Times and Seasons*, Jan. 1, 1841, 258.

in Salt Lake."[61] I wonder how many budgets, programs, policies, and decisions a General Authority has to worry about, and yet this Apostle remembered to bring stamps to a little boy across the world.

Disciples such as this aren't just loving. They notice people in the corners. They do things like regularly give an offering to the Perpetual Education Fund. They find the information for their cousins going back six generations and hurry to the temple to get their work done. They visit an elderly couple on a Sunday afternoon. They sit with the recently reactivated family during the ward Christmas party—even when their close friends have room at their table.

> And it came to pass that a Latter-day Saint man from New York City was in India on a business trip. He woke up early Sunday morning and started toward the local branch in order to partake of the sacrament. When the businessman walked into the small building where the branch met, he saw an elderly Indian woman sitting down, waiting for the meeting to begin. With a smile, the business man approached the woman, reached out his hand, and said the most unusual thing you could say to someone you've never met:
>
> "Good morning, sister."

61. Heidi S. Swinton, *To the Rescue: The Biography of Thomas S. Monson* (Salt Lake City: Deseret Book, 2010), 263.

Interruptions

3 Nephi 17:1–7

One of the things I feared most as a teenager was routine. The image of growing up, going to work, coming home, eating dinner, reading a book, and then going to bed was scary to me. I wanted to be free! I wanted to spend my life in a car following the clouds with a bottomless gas tank. I wanted to run through cornfields in Kansas and eat at some oceanside restaurant in San Francisco. Settling down meant going to prison.

I have found that it's quite liberating to have order and routine. If someone establishes a time to exercise and a time to do homework, they don't have to worry about homework while they are exercising. What good is it to be a "free spirit" if you are always thinking about what isn't done yet? President Monson has said, "Our house is to be a house of order . . . Let us provide time for family, time for work, time for study, time for service, time for recreation, time for self—but above all, time for Christ."[62] At a certain point, one realizes the need to plan and to organize around what is most important. Fred Craddock, a well-known and respected preacher said,

> How many of us defeat ourselves? When we can't play a game of
> tennis because we should be studying and we think, "I want to play

---

62. President Thomas S. Monson, "Building Your Eternal Home," *Ensign*, May 1984.

a game of tennis." Neither one is done and neither one is enjoyed because of the absence of habit.[63]

It's somewhat unusual to picture, but Jesus seems to have appointments in this chapter. After teaching the Nephites the gospel, the Sermon on the Mount, and doctrines related to the gathering of Israel, the Savior said, "Now I go unto the Father, and also to show myself unto the lost tribes of Israel" (3 Nephi 17:4). The two things the Lord had scheduled were to return to the Father and to visit the lost tribes of Israel because "they are not lost unto the Father" (3 Nephi 17:4).

However, after Jesus told the Nephites His plans, He "cast his eyes round about again on the multitude" (3 Nephi 17:5).

President Boyd K. Packer said, "The eyes of the alert teacher move constantly back and forth across the class, taking in each movement, recording each expression, responding quickly to disinterest or confusion. They read immediately a puzzled expression or sense at once when learning has taken place."[64] Effective teachers read the situation, their students, the lesson, and respond accordingly.

It seems like it would be easy to observe what students are thinking and feeling, because they give feedback through laughs, tears, nods, and smiles. In fact, I think many people believe they have a special gift for reading people. But it can be hard to focus on students when the lesson content itself requires so much attention. I was reminiscing with my students once at the end of a school year. They told me that while I was teaching one day, a student crawled through the window, went outside, and came back into the classroom. I was so lost in my lesson that I didn't notice my missing student!

Of course, the difficulty in observing extends beyond the classroom. In the routine of life, we simply stop noticing what's happening around us. For example, it's more than a little concerning to me that I can grab the car keys, start the car, stop at a red light, arrive at work, and never think about driving once. Or the couple out for their fifteenth wedding anniversary (candles, music, bread, oil, spaghetti) and the husband

---

63. Fred Craddock, *Craddock on the Craft of Preaching* (St. Louis, MI: Chalice Press, 2011), 177.

64. President Boyd K. Packer, *Teach Ye Diligently* (Salt Lake City: Deseret Book, 1975), 138–39.

doesn't realize how much it actually hurts his wife that he keeps checking the score on his cellphone.

> And it came to pass that the teenage boy came home from school, grabbed a glass from the cupboard, swung the refrigerator door open too quickly, poured the milk, took a drink, and slammed the glass on the counter too hard. The father sitting at the kitchen table asked, "How was your day?"
> "It was great," the son replied in a monotone voice.
> "Fantastic, son!" The father said as he looked at his IPAD, thinking he had connected with his boy.

The Savior had an appointment to visit the Father, but then Jesus stopped and observed. "And [he] beheld [the Nephites] were in tears, and did look steadfastly upon Him as if they would ask Him to tarry a little longer with them" (3 Nephi 17:5). Jesus demonstrated remarkable flexibility and grace in this moment by stopping and taking time to observe the people He was teaching.

But doesn't He have an appointment with the Father? I can't think of a more important meeting!

In a study performed in the 1970s, a group of future ministers at Princeton Theological Seminary were asked to give a talk on campus. Some were to speak on the Good Samaritan and some were to speak on their future opportunities as ministers. The researches told one third of the participants that they were early, one third that they were on time, and the last third that they were late for their talk. Unknown to the ministers, a person was also "planted" outside the building where the ministers were to speak. Those performing the study wanted to see who would stop and help the person who appeared to need help. "After the data was weighed and the variables analyzed, only one variable could be used to predict who would stop to help and who wouldn't. The important factor was not personality type or whether a student's career or the parable of the Good Samaritan was foremost in his mind. It was whether or not he was in a hurry."[65]

Once in early spring, I spent most of a cold day working in the back-yard while the kids were outside playing around me. Toward the end of the day, as it was getting dark, one of my sons approached me. He was only two or three at the time. His face was dirty, his nose was runny, and he was crying. My conscience told me that I should spend some time with him. Unfortunately, I picked him up, brought him downstairs, put him on the couch, and turned on a movie. I told myself that I really needed to get the yard work done, but I wished I had acted on what President Henry B. Eyring has promised: "If we pray to know what He would have us do next, He will multiply the effects of what we do in such a way that time seems to be expanded."[66]

In this chapter, the Savior had an appointment to visit the Father, but He observed the Nephites and "said unto them: Behold, my bowels are filled with compassion towards you. Have ye any that are sick among you?" (3 Nephi 17:6–7). The sick, lame, blind, dumb, and the afflicted were brought to Him. Then Jesus did *exactly* what the Father would have wanted him to do: "He did heal them every one as they were brought forth unto him" (3 Nephi 17:9).

I once had a principal who had been in the system for over twenty years when I taught with him. Our offices were right across the hall from one another. I would often walk over to his office to talk, share lesson ideas, or ask him advice about life. I loved talking to him, because I always felt welcomed and understood. His office was clean, but it was a classic seminary teacher office: full of books, maps, pictures, and little scriptural gadgets. Interestingly, when you sat across the desk from the principal, you could see an eight- by eleven-inch piece of paper taped to the wall behind him:

You are not an interruption in my life—you are the purpose for it.[67]

---

65. Judith Shulevitz, *The Sabbath World: Glimpses of a Different Order of Time* (New York: Random House, 2011), 25.

66. President Henry B. Eyring, "Education for Real Life," *Ensign*, Oct. 2002.

67. This quote is attributed to many people, one of which is Mahatma Gandhi. See helpscout.com/customer-service-quotes/famous-people/; accessed March 3, 2020.

In Our Daily Lives

3 NEPHI 25

And it came to pass that there were three suitcases by the front door. A middle-aged man walked into the kitchen and said to his daughter,

"Sweetie."

"What dad?"

"We need to talk about something."

"We are not having this conversation, Dad."

"Princess, this is your first year at BYU . . ."

"Oh my gosh, I can't believe this."

"Sweetie, there are lots of returned missionaries at BYU who are looking for a wife . . ."

"DAD! We don't need to talk about this. I'm not going to get married my freshman year. People who get married their freshman year are so weird!"

"Please don't talk about your mother and me like that. Look, I just want to make sure you don't make any . . ."

"I promise I will not get married!"

The father looked at his daughter. She repeated softly, "I promise." They packed up the car and drove past the BYU Creamery on ninth, through lots of construction (because there always seems to be construction on campus). They arrived at her new apartment, unpacked the bags, and said one more goodbye.

The following Monday, the girl's roommate told her that they were having FHE in their apartment that night. At about 7:00 p.m., five boys knocked on their door. As the girl came in from the back room to greet everyone, her eyes laid hold on one young man.

She couldn't help but smile.

Suddenly, in the distance, she heard a violin playing. Birds flew in through the window, and celestial choirs were singing.

"Hi, my name is Peter Hyrum Anderson."

"Hi, I'm Molly Emma Christensen."

A few weeks later, Molly's father and mother were in the kitchen finishing dinner when the mother noticed a call on her cell phone. She answered it and talked for a minute. With an explosion of excitement, she said, "Guess what?! Molly is getting married!"

After choosing colors, eating wedding cake, and a reception on a basketball court, the couple found themselves married.

One morning (about seven months later), Molly pulled the bathroom mirror open to get a toothbrush and she noticed the cap was off the toothpaste.

"Sweetie," said Molly, "no big deal, but do you mind putting the cap back on the toothpaste?"

A short time after, the couple was eating breakfast when Peter noticed Molly slurping her milk as she ate her cereal. "Honey," said Peter, "do you mind not slurping as you eat your cereal? No big deal."

A few years and a couple of kids later, Peter quietly left a clean house for work one morning. After ten hours of work, he came home to a house that looked like the Battle of Gettysburg.

"I'm glad you're home! It's so nice to see you! I really need your help right now!" exclaimed Molly.

"Oh, no! I feel so bad, but tonight is basketball night with the guys. Sorry, I've got to go."

Eventually, Peter and Molly began noticing that things were a little off in their marriage. Instead of seeing each other as a source of happiness, they saw each other as obstacles. In an attempt to make things better, Peter started watching videos on YouTube about effective communication. In one video, he learned that if he restated what people were saying it helps them feel understood. About a week later, when Molly and Peter were having a heated discussion in the car, Peter started restating everything that Molly was saying. "Please don't do that right now! I know what you're trying to do!" Molly said.

Fifteen years later, instead of going on a date, Peter was in the basement watching ESPN while Molly was upstairs drowning in her cellphone. Their marriage felt like a desert. No matter how many self-help books they read, goals they set, or communication techniques they tried, things never seemed to feel right.

What should they do?

I think the central problem in a situation like this is simple. Relationship advice often centers on behavior, but the real issue is the state of our hearts toward one another. As the Arbinger Institute says, "The deepest way in which we are right or wrong . . . is in our *way of being* toward others. I can be right on the surface—in my behavior . . . while being entirely mistaken beneath, in my way of being."[68]

Regardless of how I act, if my heart (or way of being) is not in the right place toward someone, something will feel off. Mormon said, "A bitter fountain cannot bring forth good water; neither can a good fountain bring forth bitter water" (Moroni 7:11). A group of people can be on the beach in Cancun, but if they don't like each other, it will feel like they are doing taxes. In contrast, friends can be in a one-bedroom apartment, and they will talk, reminisce, and laugh together the entire night.

> And it came to pass that a girl named Sophia had a crush on a boy named Matthew since seventh grade. Senior year, Sophia's friends informed Matthew about his secret crush and convinced him to ask Sophia to prom. She accepted the invitation and went to seventeen stores looking for a prom dress. Eventually, after a "day date," hair, make-up, and pictures, the limo arrived, and the group of friends went off to their final high school dance. But half way through the night, the girl sensed something was wrong. Even though the boy smiled, opened doors, and tried to make conversation, she could tell the boy wished he had gone with someone else.

Perhaps the most frightening aspect of having unkind feelings toward someone is that it happens so naturally. We live in a fallen world where the influence of Satan, if left unchecked, begins to creep in on the best relationships. What can we do to prevent this? How can we help marriages get stronger and stronger? How can a couple maintain a marriage where their hearts are filled with love?

In 3 Nephi 25, the Savior quotes the entire chapter of Malachi 4 to the Nephites. Although the first verse speaks of a time when the proud

---

68. *The Anatomy of peace* (Farmington, UT: Arbinger Institute, 2001), 57.

"shall [burn as] stubble," there is also a promise of hope in this chapter. The Lord says that He will send "Elijah the prophet" and "he shall turn the heart of the fathers to the children, and the heart of the children to their fathers" (3 Nephi 2:5–6).

If I were to ask most Latter-day Saints why someone should be married in the temple, they would probably say, "So they can be with their family forever." That's a fantastic answer, but there is another reason why temple marriage is so important. President James E. Faust once said,

> Perhaps we regard the power bestowed by Elijah as something associated only with formal ordinances performed in sacred places. But these ordinances become dynamic and productive of good only as they reveal themselves in our daily lives. Malachi said that the power of Elijah would turn the hearts of the fathers and the children to each other. The heart is the center of the emotions and a conduit for revelation. This sealing power thus reveals itself in family relationships, in attributes and virtues developed in a nurturing environment, and in loving service. These are the cords that bind families together, and the priesthood advances their development. In imperceptible but real ways, "the doctrine of the priesthood shall distil upon thy soul [and thy home] as the dews from heaven.[69]

In other words, the same power that healed the blind, raised the dead, split the Red Sea, and created worlds without number seals hearts together and makes love everlasting.

Couples who rely on the Savior's power as manifested through the sealing ordinance continue to work on their marriage, because they know that the Lord will sanctify their efforts. They don't panic just because they don't feel like newlyweds every second of every day. They don't question if they married the right person, because they know that the Lord is changing both husband and wife into the right kind of people. Instead of being an emotionally needy person focused on self, they have a heart *turned* to their spouse. Of course, these couples read scriptures, say prayers, and attend the temple together, but they don't participate in these routines because they believe they make a good marriage. Rather, these spiritual habits remind them of the only Person who can make love deep and

---

69. President James E. Faust, "Fathers, Mothers, Marriage," *Ensign*, Aug. 2004, 2–7.

authentic. Ultimately they realize that Jesus has overcome all division, pride, and enmity and is working that same miracle in their own marriage.

President Henry B. Eyring and Sister Kathleen Eyring were married in July 1962. A personal journal entry written in 2005 illustrates what a relationship can look like after many years. President Eyring wrote the following: "After dinner we watched the movie *Forever Young*, with Mel Gibson. The romantic ending is of young love reunited. The music at the end of the film, as it was in the beginning, was Billie Holiday singing 'The Very Thought of You.' We, Kathleen in tennis shoes and I without shoes, danced on the basement carpet until the last note."[70]

This couple is more than just married.

They are sealed.

---

70. President Henry J. Eyring and Robert I. Eaton, *I Will Lead You Along: The Life of Henry B. Eyring* (Salt Lake City: Deseret Book, 2013), 493.

Picturing the Future

When you think about your employment in the next ten years, what do you picture? Are you moving up the corporate ladder to an office with a big window, leather chair, and a flat-screen TV?

When you think about your children in twenty years, what do you picture? Are they dressed in robes, receiving a PhD from Yale? Or are they throwing a touchdown pass to win the college football national championship?

When you think about the word *retirement*, what do you picture? Are you on a mission in England with your spouse? Or are you on a beach with your toes in white sand, a fruit drink in your hand, and a summer hat on your head? Or maybe some kind of combination (a mission to the Caribbean)?

Let's try one more. Be open and honest with yourself. What pops into your head when you think about heaven?

Clouds? Harps? Angels?

The scriptures use powerful images to describe heaven. I'm not sure when they are literal or symbolic (I'm not too worried about it), but when you read these canonical portraits, you experience a small piece of the presence of God. For example, Revelation 22 says that heaven has a "pure river of water of life, clear as crystal, proceeding out of the throne of God" that runs next to "the tree of life, which bare twelve manner of fruits" (Revelation 22:1–2). Alma described heaven as "God sitting upon his throne, surrounded with numberless concourses of angels, in the attitude of singing and praising their God" (Alma 36:22). The prophet Joseph Smith explained that some angels "reside in the presence of God, on a globe like a sea of glass and fire, where all things for their glory are manifest, past, present, and future, and are continually before the Lord" (Doctrine and Covenants 130:7). At another time, Joseph Smith saw that heaven had a "gate . . . which was like circling flames of fire" (Doctrine and Covenants 137:2) and contained "beautiful streets . . . which had the appearance of being paved with gold" (Doctrine and Covenants 137:4).

Latter-day Saints understand heaven in a different way when compared with some traditional Christians. Orson Pratt explained that we will enjoy a *material* heaven containing "vegetation . . . animals . . . food . . . musical instruments . . . social amusements" and that we will "visit neighboring towns and worlds."[71] I'm grateful for this knowledge, because I like trees, birds, corn on the cob, violins, and baseball. It's comforting to know that earthly joys reflect heavenly ones. In fact, the scriptures are clear that this earth will eventually become celestialized (Doctrine and Covenants 88:17–18). In a very real sense, God isn't just trying to get us into heaven. He is also trying to make *this earth* heavenly.

Some may say that having an understanding of heaven ultimately doesn't matter, but people give a lot in their attempts to build the kingdom of God on earth. Relief Society presidents give a "full-time-job amount of time" for their calling. Members of the Church with very little money (or a lot) give 10 percent of their income to the kingdom. Many pioneers gave their lives with the hope of reaching Zion. Learning about heaven matters, because it helps us understand the ultimate purpose of the plan of salvation. Everything we have done and everything God has sacrificed for us is so we can enjoy the blessings of heaven.

So here is the bottom line: heaven is beautiful, filled with righteous people, material, and glorious.

---

71. Elder Orson Pratt, *Millennial Star*, vol. 28, Nov. 17, 1866, 722.

Well, sort of. There is more to the story:

> There was once a certain man that was exceedingly rich. After he retired and moved to a small town, he wanted to bring some culture to his community. He decided to rent the local auditorium so a string quartet could play a free concert. The rich man contacted the most famous and qualified musicians from all over the world to form the string quartet.
>
> Eventually, on the night of the concert, with the auditorium filled, the man approached the musicians and said, "Are you excited for tonight?"
>
> "Yes. But, we really think we should have had time to practice together first."
>
> "You'll be fine!" said the man. "You are the best musicians in the world."
>
> The four walked out on stage and sat down. The applause went silent, the spotlight centered on the first violinist, and she began to play. The three others started to play their parts. And it came to pass that the music was awful.

In 4 Nephi, heaven comes to earth. Of course, it sounds glorious and beautiful, and the people are individually righteous, but the Nephites also "had all things common among them; therefore there were not rich and poor, bond and free" (4 Nephi 1:3). They "were married, and given in marriage" (4 Nephi 1:11), or, in other words, they were organized into families. "Every man did deal justly one with another" (4 Nephi 1:2). The people continued "in meeting together oft" (4 Nephi 1:12), and "there was no contention on the land" (4 Nephi 1:15).

For the Nephites, heaven was not an individual experience.

When President Kimball was having his portrait painted, the artist asked him if he had ever been to heaven. To the artist's surprise, President Kimball said "yes" and then related a series of vignettes that provided "glimpses of heaven." One vignette recounted President Kimball visiting a stake president's home for a meal. He described watching the children (each with a different responsibility) set the tablecloth, put out knives, forks, spoons, a pitcher, and plates. The family knelt in prayer against chairs that were turned toward the table. President Kimball said, "It was most refreshing to sit with a large family where interdependence and love and harmony were visible."[72]

Some members of the Church have the opportunity to attend general conference. Besides hearing the gospel taught by living prophets and apostles, they also get to sing hymns with approximately 22,000 other Latter-day Saints. I have had that opportunity a few times in my life. It's hard to describe the feeling that is created when people from different backgrounds sing the hymns of Zion together. At one moment, people with different political views, jobs, and cultures, praise God together. Since Latter-day Saints have been singing these songs their entire lives, some sing bass, tenor, alto, or soprano. Together, they make the most beautiful music.

It is hard to describe, but I think I know the word.

---

72. President Spencer W. Kimball, "Glimpses of Heaven" *Ensign*, Dec. 1971.

Created in the Image of God

MORMON 6:17–22

It feels almost disrespectful to try to capture this moment. Mormon, the prophet-historian, is lamenting the destruction of his people. Maybe we should close the Book of Mormon, go for a walk, and pick up in the next chapter. But, of course, there is something here that we are to learn and experience.

Mormon's lament is thoughtful and poetic. He wrote the words, "O ye fair ones" (Mormon 6:17) repeatedly as he considered the "sons and daughters," "fathers and mothers," and "husbands and wives" (Mormon 6:19) that had been killed in the final Nephite battle. Besides the multiple exclamation points in our English version, scholars have noticed that the lament is written in series of parallelisms (an ancient form of poetry that repeats ideas). It seems that Mormon worked particularly hard to express what he was feeling at this devastating moment in Nephite history.

Even still, it can be difficult for us to capture what Mormon is experiencing. Humans are not good at forcing themselves to feel things. If we could, we would turn emotions on and off like a light switch. In fact, we sometimes feel manipulated when people try to get us to feel emotion. We have all witnessed the teacher whose tears seem a little forced. We have all attended events where someone tries to inspire a crowd, but it ends up feeling like a high school pep rally where no one gets "pepped." Fred Craddock said, "No matter how much a speaker pledges sincerity, shows feeling, and swears genuine concern, a direct disgorging of emotion does not reproduce that same experience in me."[73]

Besides, most people probably wouldn't *want* to experience what Mormon is feeling. I guess on some level we can't blame them—it seems like Mormon is in a lot of emotional pain.

Some might even claim that he is being slightly judgmental. Can you imagine if a modern person said, "Your sins cause me deep sorrow"?

But, I think there is something divine in Mormon's sorrow. His lament echoes Enoch's experience when "the God of heaven looked upon the residue of the people and he wept" (Moses 7:28). Enoch was so surprised to witness God crying that he asked, "How is it that thou canst weep, seeing thou art holy, and from all eternity to all eternity?" (Moses 7:29).

For a lot of the world's history, that would have been a shocking revelation of God. The Westminster Confession (a traditional Christian creed) declares, "There is but one only living and true God, who is infinite in being and perfection, a most pure spirit, invisible, *without body, parts or passions*."[74] On the other hand, for Latter-day Saints, it is central to our theology that God not only has a body but that He also has emotions, passions, and feelings. In this sense, Mormon's lament reveals to us, at least in part, what it means to be created in the image of God.

You should be warned—to experience what Mormon was feeling comes with a cost. As Terryl and Fiona Givens explained, "If love means responsibility, sacrifice, and vulnerability, then God's decision to love us is the most stupendously sublime moment in the history of time. He chooses to love even at, necessarily at, the price of vulnerability."[75]

In other words, a girl can miss a semester of college to go to a third-world country, work fifteen hours a day installing water wells, help people develop more effective farming methods, and there will still be horrific amounts of starvation on the planet.

---

73. Fred Craddock, *Overhearing the Gospel* (St. Louis: MI: Chalice Press, 2002), 106–7.

74. See apuritansmind.com/westminster-standards/chapter-2/; accessed March 3, 2020.

75. Terryl L. Givens and Fiona Givens, *The God Who Weeps: How Mormonism Makes Sense of Life* (Salt Lake City: Ensign Peak, 2012).

It means that a couple can choose to have a child, bring them bottles in the middle of the night, attend all their basketball games, drag them to church, listen to their teenaged drama, and that child may not want to spend time with them when they're adults.

It means that a missionary can study the gospel every day, be patient and kind when street contacting, refine his or her language skills, fast and pray, and never have a single baptism on his or her mission.

Some might say to Mormon, "What are you so worried about? The sins of the Nephites are not your problem. Stop mourning. Pack up your sword, helmet, shield, family, and move away. You've been through enough. You've done your part. Find a comfortable house in a comfortable neighborhood and live out your life comfortably."

Someday you'll come in from doing work in your backyard. You'll grab a book, put on some soft music, and sit down in your favorite chair. Within five minutes, you'll get a text from someone in the ward that says, "Can you come to my house for a little while? I need your help with something."

You will have a decision to make: Will you live comfortably or will you live like God?

Who Am I Really?

Jaredite kings are an interesting bunch. For the most part, they are not the kind of men you want your daughter to date. For example: Ethem. Although he "did obtain the kingdom . . . he also did do that which was wicked in his days" (Ether 11:11). During his time, "The prophets mourned and withdrew from among the people" (Ether 11:13). Plus, he named his son "Moron" (Ether 11:14).

Heth, another Jaredite king, was not much better. He "began to embrace the secret plans again" (Ether 9:26) and "did dethrone his father, for he slew him with his own sword" (Ether 9:27). The prophets were cast into pits "according to [his] commandment" (Ether 9:29) and he eventually died of starvation.

Riplakish also "did not do that which was right in the sight of the Lord" (Ether 10:5). He had concubines, taxed the people, built prisons, and sat on an "exceedingly beautiful throne" (Ether 10:6). He died in war, and his descendants were driven out of the land.

Morianton, on the other hand, is a little tricky to categorize. If he were alive today, he would have many followers on social media. First, he became king by gathering "together an army of outcasts" (Ether 10:9). For some reason, we love the idea of outcasts defeating the establishment. We watch movies about Robin Hood or the undersized football team defeating the former state champions. Morianton also "did ease the burden of the people, by which he did gain favor in the eyes of the people" (Ether 10:10). Not only do we love the outcast, we like the CEO who walks around the office shaking hands, telling stories, and laughing with his employees.

Ultimately, our favorite leaders are those who make things happen: "Morianton built up many cities, and the people became exceedingly rich under his reign, both in buildings, and in gold, and silver, and in raising grain, and in flocks, and herds" (Ether 10:12). If Morianton ran for office today, I think he would be elected.

However, Morianton is actually a complicated character. He "did do justice unto the people, but not unto himself because of his many whoredoms; wherefore he was cut off from the presence of the Lord" (Ether 10:11). It isn't surprising that Morianton is a mixture of good and bad. Most of us are a kaleidoscope of moods, history, logic, strengths, and weaknesses. Good playwrights, directors, authors, and artists recognize this fact about humans and try to incorporate it into their work. It's hard to identify with flat characters: always righteous or always wicked. Even in the scriptures, we often see the human side of prophets. Lehi murmured against God, Nephi struggled with self-doubt, Ammon had a complicated past, and the Brother of Jared hung out on the beach for four years before going to the promised land. Human beings cannot be painted with one color.

But there is something about this truth that is dangerous. Since people are complicated and make mistakes, many believe that this is what it means to be authentic. There is a feeling that if people are sinning then they are "being real."

For example, two teenagers skip Sunday School, and one says, "I have to be honest. I really really don't like that class."

Or, two friends are gossiping about someone in the ward: "Well, if you want to know my real feelings, I'm not a huge fan of hers."

Or, an eighteen-year-old at general conference looks around at all the happy, beautiful, righteous humans, and thinks, *I must be honest with myself. I could never be like these people.*

Or, a man falls in love with his secretary, leaves his wife, and asks his friends, "What do you want me to do? Lie to myself? I fell in love with another woman."

All of the people in these examples make the faulty (and very costly) assumption that if someone feels or thinks something, then it reveals who they really are.

But I've seen humans who are truly authentic, and they look much different than passing impulses. For example, in college I was once eating with a friend and noticed that his sweatshirt had the F.A.R.M.S. (Foundation of Ancient Research and Mormon Studies) logo on the front. Being a scriptural nerd, I told him that I really liked his sweatshirt. Without the least bit of self-righteousness, he took off his sweatshirt and gave it to me.

Is that what it means to be truly human?

President Brigham Young said, "Man, the noblest work of God, was in his creation designed for an endless duration, for which the love of all good was incorporated in his nature. It was never designed that he should naturally do and love evil."[76] It's true that Morianton was complicated. There were two sides to him. We get to determine which side was authentic.

Michelangelo spent about four years painting the Sistine Chapel. It contains some of the most iconic scenes in religious history: the Creation, the Fall of Adam and Eve, and the Final Judgment. When I was a kid, I learned that experts had cleaned up the Sistine Chapel in order to restore its original appearance. Over many years, the paintings had collected grime from candle smoke. I honestly feel bad for all the people who visited the chapel before it was restored to its original beauty.

I can't help but wonder how many of those visitors thought they were seeing the real thing.

---

76. President Brigham Young, *Journal of Discourses*, 9:305.

Flesh and Blood

MORONI 4–5

Moroni says that the Nephites administered the sacrament "according to the commandments of Christ" (Moroni 4:1). In other words, this ordinance was conducted in a specific manner. Only worthy priesthood holders are granted permission to prepare, pass, and bless the sacrament. In fact, if a sixteen-year-old self-conscious priest misses one word during the sacrament prayer, it must be offered again. President Dallin H. Oaks said, "The ordinance of the sacrament makes the sacrament meeting the most sacred and important meeting in the Church."[77] The most holy gathering of the Saints is not Sunday School, not bishopric meeting, not girl's camp, not general conference, but sacrament meeting.

However, it can still be difficult to make sacrament a meaningful experience. It's easy to come in through the big wooden doors, sit down on the comfortable pews, take out a green hymn book, and then just let our minds wander. Perhaps the sheer frequency of this ordinance causes us to sometimes take it for granted. If someone started taking the sacrament the week they were born and then lived until the age of seventy-five, they would take it 3,900 times. I know that we can't have 3,900 Alma the Younger experiences, but are there small ways to make sacrament a more meaningful experience?

---

77. President Dallin H. Oaks, "Sacrament Meeting and the Sacrament," *Ensign*, Nov. 2008.

I know how to make sacrament a more powerful experience: turn off your cell phone. It's too easy to double click the home screen, check the score, open up a game, or tell yourself you have to respond to a text. President Dallin H. Oaks said, "Sacrament meeting is not a time for whispered conversations on cell phones or for texting."[78] Think of what would happen to Latter-day Saint worship if no one was distracted by their cell phone.

Actually, I'm not sure that's enough.

Eliminating distractions is great, but someone could sit through sacrament, not be distracted, and still be unengaged. I think it could help to really listen to the words of the sacrament prayer and ponder their meanings. What does "always remember" mean? What does it mean to "witness" something unto God? What does it mean to "bless and sanctify this bread unto the souls"? There's enough depth in the sacrament prayers for a lifetime of contemplation. Plus, we have more than just the prayers to inspire us during the ordinance. We also have the music:

> In humility, our Savior,
> Grant thy Spirit here, we pray,
> As we bless the bread and water
> In thy name this holy day.[79]

President J. Reuben Clark Jr. said, "We get nearer to the Lord through music than perhaps through any other thing except prayer."[80] Imagine a congregation sitting up straight, singing fervently, and reverently bowing their heads and meditating on the sacrament prayer as they wait to partake of the bread and water. If that kind of worship occurred during the sacrament, the ward would turn into hot coals on a campfire.

No, this isn't enough either.

78. Oaks, "Sacrament Meeting and the Sacrament."

79. "In Humility, Our Savior," *Hymns*, no. 172.

80. President J. Reuben Clark Jr., in Conference Report, Oct. 1936, 111.

Sacrament isn't just about having a spiritual experience in church. I know how we can get more out of sacrament: the ordinance has to influence our everyday life. The way to make sacrament meaningful is to set concrete goals that improve the way we act as Christians.

When I was in a singles ward, I remember hearing a great idea during a stake conference. A member of my stake presidency said that he sets three goals every week during the sacrament. The following Sunday he then prayerfully reviews how he did with his goals. Imagine what would happen to the Church if each member set goals every sacrament meeting.

Actually, I wonder if we would become more selfish. Sometimes self-improvement is just obsession with self. Rather than thinking of how I can improve myself during sacrament, I should think of how I can improve the life of others. How powerful would sacrament be if I was always pondering ways I could bless others during the upcoming week? I could write my ideas down and then act on them.

That's really wonderful, but I can set those types of goals without going to church. I want to know how I can get more out the sacrament.

To me, it feels strange asking, "How I can get more out of sacrament?" Doing things like turning off my cell phone, pondering the prayers, singing the hymns, and setting goals would help, but in one sense it doesn't feel right asking, "How can I get more out of sacrament?"

> In a certain city, there was a man and a woman who had been married for twenty-seven years. A few days before their second daughter's wedding, the husband asked his wife, "Honey, how can I make sure that I get a lot out of this wedding?"
>
> A few months later, one of their good friends in the ward died. Dressed in black and on the way to the funeral, the husband asked his wife, "How can I really get something out of this funeral?"
>
> A few years later, shortly before the couple went to visit the husband's mother (whom they hadn't seen in four years) he asked, "How can I make sure I get something out of visiting my mom?"
>
> The wife turned to her husband and said, "Every time you have to ask that question shows that you don't really sense the importance of what's happening."

What is happening during the administration of the sacrament? Moroni tells us, "The manner of their elders and priests administering *the flesh and blood of Christ* unto the church" (Moroni 4:1). The next chapter says that when someone partakes of the sacrament, they do it in "remembrance of the blood of [God's] Son, which was shed for them" (Moroni 5:2).

Your neighbors will give you a ride to the store if your car breaks down.

Your home ministers will come by and visit with you.

Your friends will provide a listening ear.

Your family will share all of life with you.

But only one allowed His flesh to be torn and His blood to be spilt in order to pay for all your selfishness, lust, bitterness, and pride.

Although I think it is an honest and sincere question, in one sense I pray that God will forgive me for all the times I've wondered, *How can I get more out of the sacrament?*

Once, as the Savior was passing through Samaria, a group of people called out to Him saying, "Jesus, Master, have mercy on us" (Luke 13:13). The Savior told the group to go show themselves to the priests. As the ten men were walking away, their sores and scabs began to vanish. One of those lepers came back and fell at the Savior's feet in gratitude.

You can go get that leper, bring him through the big wooden doors, put him on one of those comfortable pews, and give him a green hymnbook.

He is ready.

About the Author

Stephan Taeger is a scholar of modern preaching methods, full-time religious educator, youth speaker, and presenter at BYU Education Week. He received a PhD in instructional psychology and technology from Brigham Young University. Stephan has published multiple articles related to preaching and story-based teaching techniques. He lives in Utah with his wife, Kirsten, and their six children.

Scan to visit

stephantaeger.com